PONTIFICAL INSTITUTE OF MEDIAEVAL STUDIES

STUDIES AND TEXTS

NO. 21

Figure 1. The Antiphon *Christus Resurgens* from Bodley Ms Rawl. lit. d. 4 (folio 86).

THE PROCESSIONS
OF SARUM AND
THE WESTERN CHURCH

by

Terence Bailey

PONTIFICAL INSTITUTE OF MEDIAEVAL STUDIES
TORONTO, 1971

Printed in the Netherlands by Royal Van Gorcum Ltd., Assen

ACKNOWLEDGMENT

This book has been published with the help of a grant from the Humanities Research Council of Canada, using funds provided by the Canada Council.

TO KATHRYN

TABLE OF CONTENTS

PART ONE. THE SARUM PRACTICE

Chapter

PART TWO. THE GENERAL PRACTICE

LIST OF TABLES

LIST OF ILLUSTRATIONS

INTRODUCTION

This work proposes to describe and study the ceremonies and chants of the processions of the Western Church as a whole. Why then, it might be asked, devote so much attention to an English provincial Cathedral founded only latterly in the eleventh century, when another more venerable and more central to the world's affairs might, seemingly, have been chosen? The choice is vindicated, partly by the circumstances of the liturgical practices of the Middle Ages, and partly by the special virtues of the customs of Salisbury Cathedral—or Sarum, as it is usually called.

It was not until late in the nineteenth century that there existed a standard set of service books[1] containing the ritual, prayers and chants of the Latin Church. Even today absolute uniformity is far from the rule. In the Middle Ages the Roman Rite existed in a great many regional "uses," all fundamentally similar, but each with its idiosyncrasies of detail. Of these uses one can claim a pre-eminent position. In 1256 it could be asserted that:

> Among the churches of the whole world the church of Sarum hath shone resplendent like the sun, in respect of its divine service...[2]

Moreover, the following passage will suggest that the Sarum Use had what amounted to official recognition and approbation in Rome itself:

> In ancient tymes the Catholicke Bishops of Salisbury obtayned the Titles of the Pope's Maister of the Cerimonyes, and had their places always assigned them in the Pope's Chappell and other solemnityes at Rome, according to that dignity.[3]

---

[1] The scholarly and editorial activity which produced them took place mainly at the French Abbey of Solesmes, and was begun under the leadership of Dom Prosper Guéranger. The task is not complete. Even today there is no complete edition of the Matins music.

[2] Bishop Giles de Bridport, quoted in *Statutes of the Cathedral Church of Sarum*, edd. C. Wordsworth and D. Macleane (Bath, 1883, privately printed).

[3] *Wilson's English Martyrology* (1608), p. 194.

The Sarum Use was not only universally admired, it was perhaps the most widespread of any. The See, uniting two older dioceses, was established in Salisbury in 1075, but in spite of this late date Sarum was to have a greater influence in the matter of liturgical customs than any other single church in Europe. Sarum's Use—because of the excellence of her ritual and the correctness of her service books—was adopted increasingly by other dioceses until, in the middle of the fifteenth century, it had spread through most of England, Wales and Ireland, much of Scotland, and even to the Continent. Sarum could scarcely exhibit better credentials. No other church can claim to serve better as an exemplar. But there are still other considerations which speak in her favour.

Time, the impartial leveller, has been lenient. Sarum's is the only extant fully-rubricated processional of the Middle Ages. And there survives as well the full complement of related service books—missals, graduals, breviaries, antiphoners, ordinals—to supplement it and provide the necessary background. Another advantage—for a study intended to treat the processions in a context larger than the local—is that the Sarum customs, whether to further their influence or to accommodate the other churches which had already adopted them, were written up, even in the earliest sources, in such a way as to be general in their application. There is no question that the ceremonies were drawn up originally with Salisbury Cathedral in mind. There are numerous references in the rubrics of the Processional to Sarum and to features of its topography. But directions are usually left indefinite where—had there only been the Cathedral to consider—they might have been specific. This can be seen in the following excerpts:

Hoc eodem modo fiat processio in omnibus festis majoribus et dominicis contingentibus et in festo Annunciationis et Conceptionis beate Marie in quacumque feria celebratur viz apud Sarum et in locis ubi dedicata est ecclesia in honore beate Marie...

The same is to be done for the procession on Major Double feasts and coincident Sundays, and—at Sarum and in places where the church is dedicated to blessed Mary—on the feasts of Annunciation and Conception.

Hic fiat prima stacio viz ex parte ecclesie boriali in extrema parte occidentali hoc est ad ecclesiam Sancte Marie Sarum ante crucem in septentrionali cimiterio.[1]

Here is held the first station, that is, on the north side of the church at the extreme west end; at the church of St. Mary of Sarum this is in front of the cross in the north cemetery.

[1] Bodley, Ms Rawl. lit. d. 4, f. 12, 44v.

It is quite certain that the formulation of the rubrics in general terms was deliberate, and this can be shown by comparing the directions in the Processional with their counterparts in a manuscript written specifically for use in the Cathedral. Ms 148 of the Salisbury Chapter Library[1] is not a processional, and not entirely a service book. But it does contain directions and prayers for the conclusion in the choir of some of the processions, and for some of the related ceremonies. Following are given, one after the other, rubrics from this book and from the Processional for the lenten ferial processions and for the washing of the altars on Holy Thursday:

Eat processio per ostium presbiterii septentrionale ad altare sancte Martini ex parte ecclesie boriale.[2]	The procession shall go through the north door of the presbytery to the altar of St. Martin on the north side of the church.
Exeat, primo, processio per ostium presbiterii boriale, ad unum altare ex eius latere.[3]	The procession shall set out first of all through the north door of the presbytery to one of the altars on that side.
Post prandium veniant clerici ad altaria abluenda, sed in primis benedicatur aqua more dominicali ad altare sancti Nicholai privatim.[4]	After lunch the clerks shall return for the washing of the altars, but first water is blessed as on Sundays, privately, at the altar of St. Nicholas.
Post prandium conveniant clerici ... ad altaria abluenda ... In primis benedicatur aqua more dominicali ex chori privatim scilicet in vestibulo ante altare.[5]	After lunch the clerks shall assemble ... for the washing of the altars ... First water is blessed as on Sundays, privately, outside the choir in the sacristy.

Similarly, where the Processional makes no specific provisions, Ms 148, for Holy Thursday, gives directions and prayers for the washing of each of the Sarum altars by name; and for the Purification, directions which include the size of the candles to be carried during the ceremonies by each of the officers of the Cathedral—who are also named.

It should be said that the modification of the Sarum customs for general use was not completely carried out. The Processional contains certain provisions—given without option—that are justified and appro-

---

[1] Edited by C. Wordsworth in *Ceremonies and Processions of the Cathedral Church of Salisbury* (Cambridge, 1901).

[2] Ms 148, f. 24.

[3] Ms Rawl. lit. d. 4, f. 32v.

[4] Ms 148, f. 28v.

[5] Ms Rawl. lit. d. 4, f. 53v.

priate only where the church was dedicated, as was Sarum, to the Virgin. Inconsistencies for one or two feasts, like those for Annunciation and Conception which will be discussed below, were minor, and easily corrected. But the failure to take account of a different dedication had one important and far-reaching result which changed the character of the processions in most of the local churches. On the Continent the chants and prayers of the last stage of the processions were usually in honour of the patron of the church. This is clear from many processionals and other service books. At Sarum, in keeping with this general practice, the last antiphon or respond, versicle and prayer were in most processions devoted to Mary—the Cathedral's patroness. But none of the churches which adopted the Sarum customs seems to have substituted chants and prayers of their own patron. In many places the processions became—in part, at least—supernumerary Marian devotions.

It will, at this point, be clear to the reader that this study is very much concerned with the historical development of the Liturgy—a subject usually left to liturgists. But the Chant, if it is to be understood at all, cannot be divorced from its setting. Willi Apel has said:

> ... that a knowledge of the Roman liturgy ... is an indispensable prerequisite for any study of Gregorian chant, not only from the historical but also from stylistic and aesthetic points of view. It may be possible to examine or listen to a chant like the Gradual *Haec dies* and to admire its beauty without even knowing what a Gradual is nor to which feast this particular one belongs. A full understanding, however, of its form, its style, its musical values and significance cannot be gained without a knowledge of its liturgical function, and its relationship to other chants. To consider Gregorian chant as a "purely musical" discipline would involve the student in the same difficulties which, for a long time and occasionally even now, have beset philologists who considered the songs of the troubadours and Minnesingers as a "purely literary" affair, completely disregarding their intimate connection with music.[1]

There has been, to date, no considerable study of the processions or of their music. Scattered writings appear as early as 1607 with Serrarius' *Sacri Peripatetici*, and can be found in the major liturgical journals, dictionaries and encyclopedias. But they either treat the processions cursorily, in general descriptive terms, or fix their attention upon exceptional examples—such as the processions for Palm Sunday and the Feast of Corpus Christi—with features of local origin and special dramatic interest. The texts of the Sarum Processional and other service books and documents were published by W. G. Henderson, W. H. Frere, Chr.

[1] *Gregorian Chant* (Bloomington, 1958), p. 6.

Wordsworth, F. Proctor, D. Rock and others as a result of the renewal of interest, beginning about the middle of the nineteenth century, in the ritual and ancient practices of the Church in England. The editions are invaluable; but the editors were not primarily concerned with the processions. Discussions of them are kept to a minimum, and some rather obvious errors were allowed to stand. Henderson, for example, even though he edited the Processional,[1] could write, incorrectly, that there were processions at Sarum before Mass on the first three days following Easter and Pentecost.[2] All of the English scholars who talked about the processions seemed to have believed that the processions on Easter and Pentecost remained within the church and cloister. This last misunderstanding was, by the way, perpetuated recently by Frank Harrison in his *Music in Medieval Britain*.[3]

The music of the processions has been almost completely ignored, in editions, by theorists and by historians. The English liturgist William Maskell wrote in 1844 that, "music does not form, except in an extended and improper sense, any part of what we ought to understand by the term 'use' of a church."[4] Henderson, apparently in agreement with this line of thinking, included none of the melodies in his edition. Aurelian of Réomé, in the ninth century, did not think the processional antiphons "worth the trouble to include" in his extensive treatise on the chants.[5] And a thousand years later, Peter Wagner in his lengthy study[6]—although unaware, perhaps, of the size of the body of chants he was passing over in so few words—devoted to them little more than a paragraph.

This study falls into two main sections, the first concerned with the Sarum customs, the second with the general practice. Included in part I is,

I. a description and comparison of all the remaining Sarum Processionals,

II. a detailed description of the processions themselves—taken from the rubrics of the service books,

---

[1] *Processionale ad usum insignis et preclarae Ecclesiae Sarum* (Leeds, 1882).

[2] *Ibid.*, xi.

[3] London, 1958, p. 90. The occasions and route of the processions are set out below in the third chapter.

[4] *The Ancient Liturgy of the Church of England*, page x.

[5] "Letaniarum atque Rogationum caeterasque huiusmodi non operae pretium arbitratus sum huic inferere operi" (*Musica Disciplina*, ed. by Martin Gerbert in *Scriptores... de Musica* [1784], I, 54).

[6] *Einführung in die gregorianischen Melodien* (in 3 vols., third edition, Leipzig, 1911) I, 158.

III. a discussion of the chants and prayers—demonstrating the role of the music in the processions and its relationship to the Liturgy, and a transcription of all of the special Sarum processional music,

IV. an account of the history and development of the processions and their music from the founding of the Cathedral to the Reformation.

Part II of the study demonstrates the universality of the Sarum customs, discusses local differences, outlines the earliest history of the customs and music, and includes an examination of the processional musical repertory of the whole of the Western Church—Sarum's included.

The postponement of the study of the Sarum processional chants until the last chapters requires a word of explanation. The Sarum Processions are for the most part admirably representative of the general practice. But there is one important exception, and that is that the Use retained but a fraction of the special music which had in earlier centuries been associated with the processions. The large part of the total repertory is recoverable, and is discussed in this work. And as individual pieces of plainchant seldom reveal their significant features except in relation to others of the same family, it has been necessary to defer the analysis of the Sarum pieces and treat them as part of the repertory as a whole.

The order of presentation in this study offers the advantage of an immediate acquaintance with the processions in their fully-developed form—something available only in a Sarum source—an acquaintance which provides for the reader uninitiated in the complexities of the Liturgy the indispensable background for the discussion of the local variations and the historical development of the customs.

In the musical examples the eighth-note has been employed as the basic unit of the chant. An *x* in place of a note-head (♪) represents a quilisma, a short horizontal stroke through the note-stem (♪) a liquescent, a small superscript *o* (♪) an oriscus. All notes written together under a beam belong to the same syllable:

Ex. 1.

Cle-men-tis- si- me

To indicate pitches in the text *c, d, e*, etc., have been used for the octave below middle C; and *c', d', c'', d''*, etc. for the octaves above.

The spelling of the Latin presented a problem. As a rule it has been written as it would appear in classical writings, except that the medieval "e" has been retained for the diphthong "ae." It has not always been possible to settle the question of the interchangeability of *i* and *j*, nor *c* and *t*. Quotations from editions are, of course, as the editors gave them.

In keeping with recent practice all Latin passages have been provided with translations, the only exceptions being isolated phrases where the meaning is obvious, or where the point of the quotation depends upon some grammatical or lexical interpretation.

PART ONE:

THE SARUM PRACTICE

I. THE SARUM PROCESSIONALS

There are more than twenty manuscript Sarum Processionals, or frag-
ments, and at least twenty-five printed editions. But all of these manuscripts and editions are copies, abridgements, or slight modifications of
the same book. All contain—although some less completely—virtually
the same processional customs. Following is a general description of the
contents of the manuscripts comparing them to a processional in the
Bodleian Library, Oxford, Ms Rawl. liturg. d. 4. This is the most
complete of the manuscripts. It offers the closest textual agreement with
the official printed editions of the sixteenth century, but contains none of
their late additions. A marginal note, "Iste liber pertinet Ecclesie Johannis Evangeliste Dublin"[1] (This book belongs to the Church of St. John
the Evangelist, Dublin), makes it clear that Rawl. liturg. d. 4 was used
in Ireland, but there is almost no local adaptation. What there was—the
addition of a prayer to St. Anne, presumably to be used in a Vespers
procession to her altar, and the appending of processional services for
St. Patrick and St. Audoen—has been kept separate by the copyist in the
margin and at the end of the book.[2]

There are, roughly speaking, two kinds of manuscript processional.
Some are complete. These contain the whole of the liturgy—chants,
texts, and directions—for the processions, and for the services associated
with them; and in addition, a number of services and individual items
(antiphons, responds, tropes, hymns, lections, prayers) not connected
with processions at Sarum. This extra material, chiefly for Holy Week,
was doubtless included because of the convenient portability of the books.
This content varied in the manuscripts and in the editions.

Many of the manuscripts are abridgements of the Processional; in them
rubrics are reduced to a minimum, and items not required for the pro-

---

[1] Folio 189 v.

[2] The Sarum Use was evidently followed very closely in Dublin. The total adaptation in a
Sarum Consuetudinary used at St. Patrick's Cathedral in the fourteenth century consists of the
added words, "et eadem in ecclesie Dublin" (and the same in the Church in Dublin). See
Frere, *The Use of Sarum*, I xxvi, li.

cessions themselves, for example, blessings, lections, and stational Masses, are generally omitted. These short processionals would have to be supplemented on occasion with other service books.

The physical descriptions of the manuscripts and other information it seemed unnecessary to include here can be found in published catalogues. Nearly all of the Sarum sources are treated by Frere in his *Bibliotheca Musico-liturgica*.[1] Most of the information in the following pages has not previously been available.

The Bodleian Library

Ms Bodl. 637 (2024).[2] This is a full Processional. A leaf is missing after folio 41 with part of the Palm Sunday service. Added to the *sanctorale* are a prayer for a procession at Vespers to the altar of St. Anne, and a service for the Discovery of St. Stephen. At the end of the manuscript is a version of the hymn *Salve festa dies* for feasts of the Cross.

Ms Selden Supra 37 (3415). This is a fragment only, breaking off after the prayer *Aeternam* of the blessing of the incense on Holy Thursday. It omits the ceremony of the Boy Bishop of Vespers of the Feast of the Holy Innocents, the blessing of the salt and water, and everything for Maundy Thursday except the responds sung during the washing of the altars.

Ms Rawl. liturg. e.45 (15838). This is an abridged Processional. The provisions for the washing of the altars on Maundy Thursday are specifically for altars dedicated to St. Lawrence, St. Mary, St. James, and St. Nicholas. Processions on the feasts of St. Andrew and St. Nicholas are prescribed even in Lent. Three of the usual Palm Sunday antiphons, *Cum audisset, Ante sex dies passionis, Ante sex dies sollenitatis*, are omitted. The *sanctorale* leaves out St. Agnes, the Octave of Saints Peter and Paul, the Decollation of John the Baptist, St. Margaret, St. Edward, St. Brice, the two Saint Edmunds, and a number of the usual Vespers processions. The late feasts, Visitation, Transfiguration, and Holy Name, are included.

Ms Rawl. liturg. e.46 (15843). This is an abridged Processional, although it does include votive Masses. The manuscript has lost folios with part of the Maundy ceremony, part of the votive processions ("causa neccesi-

---

[1] For the Plainsong and Medieval Music Society (2 vols., 1901-1932).

[2] These numbers refer to the Bodleian *Summary Catalogue* (7 vols., Oxford, 1922-1953).

tatis"), and, at the end, part of the burial service. St. Anne is not included in the *sanctorale*.

Ms Rawl. liturg. e. 47 (15844). This is a fragment of an abridged Processional. It opens in the Palm Sunday service, and breaks off after the procession for St. Edward the King. The *sanctorale* omits St. Agatha, and adds processions for St. James and the Discovery of St. Stephen.

Ms Rawl. liturg. d. 4 (15846). One leaf is missing (after folio 91) with part of a psalm for the Easter Vespers procession; another leaf, which may have held services for additional Irish saints, is missing at the end. Inserted just after the *temporale* (folio 128-132) is an Easter liturgical drama. This and the Sarum ceremony of the Deposition of the Cross are discussed by Young, *The Drama of the Medieval Church* (Oxford, 1933, in 2 vols.) I, 347, 145.

Ms liturg. 6 (30595). This is an abridged Processional. Omitted from the *sanctorale* are the processions for Conception and the Octave of the Assumption; added are processions for Saints Sebastian and Fabian at Vespers to their altar, for the Translation of St. Martin, and the Discovery of St. Stephen. A prose is included for the processional respond of St. Kathrine.

Ms liturg. 408 (30622). An abridged Processional. It provides for none of the Vespers processions of the saints, nor for those of the feasts of the Cross. Omitted from the *temporale* are the processions for St. Sylvester, Corpus Christi, and everything for Ash Wednesday. The *sanctorale* omits St. Brice; added is a procession for the Discovery of St. Stephen. The manuscript provides for processions before Mass for St. Andrew and St. Nicholas in Lent.

Ms liturg. d.3 (31378). This manuscript contains two folios from a Sarum Processional, with the verse of the respond *Christus resurgens*, and part of the Easter hymn *Salve festa dies*.

Ms lat. liturg. e.7 (32704). An abridged Processional. A leaf is missing after folio 11 with part of the Christmas Week ceremonies; the *temporale* breaks off at Corpus Christi; the *sanctorale* begins only with St. Agnes, and breaks off at St. Cecelia, omitting St. Luke and St. Brice, and adding a procession for the Discovery of St. Stephen. Appended in the same hand (f. 109v) is a *Salve festa dies* for St. George, and a reference to Henry V (reigned 1413-1422) and London.

St. Edmund's Hall

Ms. 1. An abridged Processional. Omitted from the *sanctorale* are Saints John and Paul, and St. Brice; added are the Discovery of St.

Stephen, St. Bartholomew, and a prayer for a procession at Vespers to an altar of St. Anne.

The British Museum

Ms Harl. 2942. An abridged Processional with several gaps. This manuscript provides for none of the ordinary Vespers processions. Part of the *sanctorale* is missing, but the Annunciation, St. Margaret, St. Edward the King, St. Brice, and the two Edmunds were not included. The procession for St. Anne is not in place, but appended in the same hand at the end of the *sanctorale*. There is a later addition of a procession for St. Thomas of Hereford.*

Ms Harl. 2945. A full Processional. The opening of the manuscript, with everything up to the vigil of Christmas, is missing; another gap after folio 80 accounts for the loss of the services from the Rogation Days to Corpus Christi. Saints Philipp and James, St. Dunstan, St. George, and St. Vitalis are omitted from the *sanctorale*; added are the Translation of St. Swithin, the Translation of St. Martin, and Saints Simon and Jude. The processional respond for St. Kathrine is provided with a trope.

Ms add. 47663. This is a leaf from a Sarum Processional with part of the procession for the Assumption. It contains the end of the antiphon *Ascendit Christus*, all of *Anima mea*, and all of *Descendi in ortum*.

Lambeth Palace

Ms 438. This is a full Processional but without the ceremony of the Boy Bishop. Omitted from the *sanctorale* are St. Dunstan, St. Anne, and St. Brice. St. Matthew appears twice, but this is probably a copyist's error; no chants or prayers are provided for the second time. For the Feast of the Translation of St. Edward the usual Sarum respond from the Common of the Saints is replaced with a special one. The last pages of the book (folio 179v-180v) contain polyphonic litanies for the Rogation Days. (A name, perhaps the composer's, appears twice in the forms "dñdy" and "Willam (sic) dũdy.")

Jesus College

Ms 62. This is a fragment of a full Processional; the pages are bound

---

* Saints so marked were not in the Sarum Calendar.

in the wrong order, but they contain most of the material from Palm Sunday to the end of the *temporale*.

Caius College

Ms 436. An abridged Processional. Omitted from the *sanctorale* are St. Vitalis, Saints Philipp and James, St. John at the Latin Gate, St. Dunstan, Saints John and Paul, and the Decollation of St. John the Baptist.

St. John's College

Ms 151. An abridged Processional. Omitted from the *sanctorale* are the Conception, Annunciation, St. George, St. Vitalis, Saints Philipp and James, St. Brice; included is the feast of the Visitation, and an extra respond (*Quatuor animalia*) for the procession of St. Matthew.

Ms 268. This is a full Processional. The *sanctorale* is very much expanded to include the Translation of St. Edmund the King,* St. Aldhelm, St. Augustine of the English, the Translation of St. Edmund the Bishop, St. Barnabas, the Translation of St. Richard, the Translation of St. Edward (King and Martyr?), St. Alban, the Translation of St. Martin, the Translation of St. Benedict, the Translation of St. Swithin, the Discovery of St. Stephen, St. Bartholomew, St. Giles the Abbot, the Translation of St. Cuthbert, St. Edith, St. Maurus, St. Jerome, St. Rheims, St. Thomas of Hereford,* St. Francis, St. Wulstan, Saints Crispin and Crispinian, Saints Simon and Jude, St. Leonard the Abbot, St. Machutus, St. Hugh Bishop and Confessor. As in Ms 151 above, there are two responds provided for the procession of St. Matthew.

DUBLIN

Archbishop Marsh Library

Ms Z 4.2.20. This is a full Processional. It belonged, like the Bodleian Ms Rawl. liturg. d.4, to the Church of St. John the Evangelist, Dublin. This is stated explicitly on folio 141. The first folio, with part of the blessing of the salt and water, has been torn away. This book, unlike its sister, adapts the Sarum customs somewhat. Omitted from the *sanctorale* are the services for the feasts of St. John at the Latin Gate, St. Dunstan, St. Peter in Chains, and St. Hyppolitus. Added to the *sanctorale*, in place, are processions for St. Patrick, St. Columba, and St. Stephen— this last apparently for a date between September 8 and 14. The Sarum processions at Vespers are omitted for St. Margaret, and for the two

Edmunds; but similar ones are added for St. Stephen and for the Feast of Saints John and Paul. This processional contains the same Easter liturgical drama as is found in Ms Rawl. lit. d. 4, but in place, with the other Easter services. The usual short ceremony it replaced has been relegated to the end of the book. Appropriate versions of the *Salve festa dies* are given for the processions of St. Patrick, St. Columba, St. John the Baptist, and the Assumption.

EDINBURGH

National Library of Scotland

Ms 18.5.20. A full Processional, but with pages missing with part of the material for the processions for Circumcision and Epiphany, and part of the Maundy service. A whole quire has been removed with most of the Easter ceremonies. The book omits the ceremony of the Boy Bishop and the procession for St. Brice. This manuscript follows the practice of the Old Ordinal in providing alternative responds for the return of the procession to the choir on Sexagesima and Quinquagesima Sundays.

LIVERPOOL

Liverpool City Museum

Ms M 12034 (on indefinite loan to the Liverpool University Library). This is an abridged Processional, with the first pages lost. The manuscript begins with the latter part of the procession for the second Sunday of Advent. Added to the *sanctorale* is a procession for the Discovery of St. Stephen. A flyleaf (folio 188v) contains a simple four-part setting for the *Nunc dimittis* canticle.

STONYHURST

Stonyhurst College

Ms 41 (A VI 37). This is a full Processional except for blessing service for the palms and the stational Masses. The *sanctorale* omits processions for Conception, Conversion of St. Paul, Relics Day, Translation of St. Thomas, St. Anne, St. Matthew, and St. Luke; added is a procession for St. Chad, apparently the patron of the church where this manuscript was used.

It is not difficult to find reasons for the abridgement of the Processional. Such a book would be, in most circumstances, entirely adequate. A number of processional ceremonies, particularly those requiring the participation of a bishop, would never be needed in parish churches. Even in the Cathedrals, little more than the chants would be required of a processional intended for a member of the choir.

Perhaps some of the omissions in the processionals were unintentional. It is unlikely that any church would fail to celebrate Corpus Christi[1] or the Feast of St. Sylvester. Moreover, not all of the deficiencies would have mattered in practice, as a number of the missing saints could have had processions made up from the *Commune sanctorum*. However, some of the omissions in the *sanctorale* of the processionals are a result of variations in the Calendar, instances of Sarum feasts which were not celebrated locally or at least not with sufficient solemnity to warrant processions. There was certainly a difference of opinion about the Feast of Saints John and Paul and the Feast of St. Brice, whose procession is the most often omitted. In the New Ordinal these are among the occasions for which the choir was ruled; but later, in the printed Breviary of 1531, they are listed as feasts "sine regimine chori." According to the Ordinal these feasts would be celebrated with processions; according to the Breviary they would not. There was similar uncertainty about the Octave of Corpus Christi. The 1517 and later editions of the Processional preface the service for this occasion with a note: "ubi octavae habentur cum regimine chori" ([for churches] where octaves are held with a ruled choir).

In churches not dedicated to the Virgin there would be no need to include the feasts of Conception or Annunciation in the processional. Both are feasts of the third highest classification, which ordinarily would receive processions only on Sunday; and both fall in periods when the dominical service was not displaced: Conception on December 8, in Advent, and Annunciation on March 25, either in Lent or Eastertide.

The addition to the *sanctorale* of processions for local saints requires no explanation. However most of the additions in the manuscripts involved saints already in the Sarum calendar. Customarily, the Processional omitted services for many saints whose processions were expected to be made up nonetheless from the *Commune Sanctorum*. In only one of the manuscripts[2] is the *sanctorale* anything like complete. Perhaps to include

---

[1] At least, not at the end of the fourteenth century.
[2] Ms 268 of St. John's College, Cambridge.

them specifically although unnecessarily was a distinction for saints locally popular.

The case of the Discovery of St. Stephen is quite different. This is a Sarum feast which had proper responds. Its procession could not have been made up from the *Commune*. Nevertheless, it is absent from the official printed Processionals and from most of the manuscripts. Where it has been added it should be considered a correction.

A few of the feasts in the processionals were late additions to the Calendar. Saint Anne's was adopted in 1383,[1] having been ordered for England by Urban VI in order to popularize the marriage of Anne of Bohemia to Richard III.[2] The Feast of the Visitation, although celebrated from 1263 by the Franciscans, was adopted in England generally only after 1480[3].

The Feast of the Transfiguration, although it too can be found earlier in England,[4] was not proclaimed for the whole Church until 1457.[5] The Feast of the Holy Name of Jesus was ordered for Franciscans in 1530, and for the Universal Church in 1721;[6] but this feast and the Transfiguration were both adopted generally in England in the late fifteenth century. The printed supplements to the Breviaries and Missals published after 1480 contain them as "nova festa."[7]

The *Processionale Sarum* was printed as early as 1502, and continued to be issued at least until 1558. Wordsworth lists the known printed copies in his *Salisbury Processions and Ceremonies*,[8] and there, twenty-five editions can be distinguished, from London, Rouen, Paris, and Antwerp. In 1882, Henderson, believing it to be the earliest, reprinted the text of the 1508 edition,[9] collating with it the editions of 1517, 1528, 1544, and 1554, and partly, those of 1523, 1525, 1528, and 1532.

Most of the editions contain woodcuts illustrating the ceremonies.

---

[1] Wilkins, *Concilia Magnae Britaniae et Hiberniae* (1737), III, 178.

[2] H. M. Bannister, "The Introduction of the Cultus of St. Anne into the West" in *English Historical Review*, XVIII (1903), 107-112.

[3] *The Oxford Dictionary of the Christian Church* (ODCC), ed. Cross (London 1957), 1426; Wilkins, *op. cit.*, III, 613.

[4] F. Wormold, *English Benedictine Calendars* (publications of the Henry Bradshaw Society for 1938 and 1946), I, 41; II, 34.

[5] ODCC, 1371.

[6] *Ibid.*, 937.

[7] See Proctor and Wordsworth, *Breviarium ... Sarum* (3 vols., Cambridge, 1879-1886), III, li.

[8] Cambridge, 1901, pp. 328-330.

[9] Leeds, M'Corquodale and Company.

There are two sets of diagrams. The editions of 1502, 1508, and 1528 have twelve:

1. Benedictio Aquae diebus Dominicis (The Sunday blessing of the Holy Water),
2. Statio in die cinerum dum episcopus ejiciat poenitentes (The ejection of the penitents on Ash Wednesday),
3. Statio dum benedicuntur rami in dominica Ramis Palmarum (The Palm Sunday blessing of the branches),
4. Statio dum benedicitur ignis in Vigilia Paschae (The Holy Saturday blessing of the new fire),
5. Statio dum benedicitur cereus paschalis in Vigilia Paschae (The Holy Saturday blessing of the Paschal Candle),
6. Statio dum cantatur letania ad fontes in vigilia paschae (The singing of the Litany at the font on Holy Saturday),
7. Statio et ordo processionis in die Paschae ante matutinas cum cruce (The station and procession with the Cross on Easter before Matins),
8. Statio ad fontes in hebdomada Paschae (The station at the font at Vespers during Easter Week),
9. Ordo processionis in secunda feria in Rogationibus (The procession for Rogation Monday),
10. Statio et ordo processionis in die Ascensionis Domini ante missam (The station and procession before Mass on Ascension),
11. Statio ad vesperas ante crucem in sabbatis per aestatem (The station before the Cross at Vespers during the summer),
12. Statio dum benedicuntur luminaria in Purificatione beatae Mariae (The blessing of the candles on Purification).

Thirteen illustrations are found in the editions of 1519, 1523, 1525, 1530 (Paris, Nic. Prevost), and all the later editions with diagrams. Added was an illustration of the procession before Mass on Christmas (Ordo processionis in die Nativitatis Domini ante missam). The earlier set, and the diagram which was not found in the earlier set, are reproduced in both the Henderson and the Wordsworth publications.

All the editions contain the feasts of Transfiguration, Visitation, and Holy Name. All provide for a procession for the Sunday within the Octave of Corpus Christi.

II. THE FORM AND OCCASIONS
OF THE PROCESSIONS

The earliest Sarum Processionals prescribe processions for all Sundays of the year, and on the following feasts no matter what day of the week they occurred:

Christmas	Assumption
Epiphany	Relics Day
Purification	Nativity ⌐ BVM ?
Easter	All Saints
Ascension	the Feast of the Patron
Pentecost	Conception
Corpus Christi	Annunciation.
Dedication Day	

If this list were taken from the latest Processionals it would include the feasts of the Visitation, Holy Name, and Transfiguration.

All of these but Conception and Annunciation were principal or major doubles, that is, feasts of the two highest liturgical ranks.[1] The two exceptions were celebrated with extra dignity at Sarum as feasts of the patroness—the Cathedral was dedicated to the Virgin. Churches following the Sarum Rite but not dedicated to Mary probably treated Conception and Annunciation strictly according to their rank.

On all Sundays the procession was preceded by the blessing of salt and water, and the Asperges, the sprinkling of the High Altar and all the worshippers in the church. On ordinary Sundays the blessing took place at the choir-step, after Prime and Chapter. The hebdomadary priest (most large churches had several priests in attendance; the duty of officiating was rotated among them) was assisted by a deacon, a sub-deacon carrying a text of the gospel, a thurifer, two taperers, an acolyte carrying a cross, and two boys, one to carry the salt and water, and the other to hold the book the priest read from. The boys wore surplices, all the others, albs. Over his alb the priest wore a red silk cope; his ministers added amices.

---

[1] "Double" refers to the most important feasts. The origin of the term is uncertain.

On those Sundays when a double feast was celebrated, and on Palm Sunday, the blessing was carried out without ceremony at one of the side altars. On such days the proceedings were longer and more complex; it may have been felt that an elaborate service for the blessing took too much time.

The Asperges took place after Prime and Chapter on ordinary Sundays and on Pentecost; but when a double feast was celebrated and on Palm Sunday it was later—according to some manuscripts and editions of the Processional after Tierce, in others, after Sext.[1] Rubrics describe the ceremony:[2]

> After the blessing of the salt and water, let the priest go up to the main altar and sprinkle it on all sides. On his return, he shall sprinkle: first, his assistants in order, beginning with the acolyte who carries the cross; then, at the choir-step, the clerks who shall come to him there one at a time, those more senior, first; afterwards the people on both sides of the presbytery.

During the service the choir sang an antiphon; afterwards the priest sang a versicle and prayer.

The Normal Procession

The dominical procession was made up as follows:

> First, the verger, making way for the procession; then a boy in a surplice, carrying Holy Water; next the acolyte carrying the cross; and after him two taperers, walking side by side; then the thurifer; and after him the sub-deacon [carrying the text of the Gospel] and deacon—all in albs with amices, without tunicles or chasubles; and after the deacon, the

---

[1] It would appear from the Ordinal that it was the earlier practice to have the Asperges after Tierce:

Si fuerit duplex festum... hora sexta cantata aspergatur; sed nuper post terciam aspergatur ... secundum antiquum ordinale et ordinale Welbyk. (British Museum Ms Harl. 2911, folio 107.)	On a double feast the Asperges is after Sext, but formerly, according to the Old Ordinal and the Welbyk Ordinal, after Tierce.

The question was never settled.

[2] The descriptions in this chapter are based closely on the rubrics in the Processional (Bodley, Ms Rawl. lit. d. 4). It was thought unnecessary to reproduce the Latin, which is essentially the same as that of the published Processionals and available in W. G. Henderson's edition (Leeds, 1882) and, substantially, in Wordsworth's *Salisbury Processions and Ceremonies* (Cambridge, 1901) and W. H. Frere's *The Use of Sarum* (Cambridge, 1898-1901).

priest, similarly dressed, but with a silk cope; then the boys and the clerks of the second rank, not two by two, but in two groups as they are disposed in choir; and the clerks of the higher rank, those of highest dignity last, in the same order as they are disposed at chapter — [all] in ordinary habits.

The Processional prescribes a more impressive ceremony for double feasts. Three crosses were carried for feasts of the highest rank; two for minor doubles. There was an extra thurifer, and an extra Gospel text carried by the deacon. The sub-deacon and deacon wore tunicles and dalmatics; the boys and clerks all wore silk copes.

The Processional's rubrics are not always as complete as a modern reader could wish, but other Sarum books, the Customary and the Ordinal, give additional information. The Processional is deficient especially with regard to vestments. It prescribes albs for the choir on double feasts. But as it is given elsewhere that the boys and clerks wore surplices in choir from the Vigil of Easter until the end of its Octave, from the Vigil of Pentecost until the end of the Octave, on all double feasts from Easter until the Feast of St. Michael, and on the octaves of Assumption and Nativity, it is clear that surplices would be worn in any processions. The ordinary choir habit included a black cope. The choir rulers always wore surplices and silk copes, and walked immediately behind the priest. The verger was probably vested in a surplice, as this is the only dress ever prescribed for him. In keeping with the veiling of the church images which was customary on the first Monday of Lent, the processional cross on all the lenten Sundays but the first was of wood, without a crucifix.

On ordinary Sundays the procession went out, singing, through the north door of the choir and circled the presbytery — the priest sprinkling each of the altars along the way — then down the south aisle of the church, returning past the font to the rood. On double feasts the altars were not sprinkled. The procession left the choir by the west door and included the cloister.

The procession halted under the rood with the boy carrying Holy Water and the cross bearer (or bearers) standing at the rood-step at the western entrance to the choir. On Sundays from Septuagesima to Quadragesima the verse of the processional chant was sung at the rood-step by two junior clerks in choir habits, facing the people. Similarly, on Sundays from the Octave of Easter until the Sunday before Ascension the verse was sung by three clerks of the higher rank in surplices; and on Easter, from the *pulpitum*, by three senior clerks in silk copes. When the processional antiphon or respond was finished—and, during part of the year, after an antiphon, versicle and prayer had been sung before the rood—the priest turned to the people to say the Bidding Prayers. On double feasts, on the Sunday within the Octave of Christmas, and on Palm Sunday, the procession halted at the rood only long enough to finish the processional chant.

On Christmas and on the Feast of St. Thomas the prose to the processional respond was sung by three senior clerks in silk copes; similarly on St. Stephen's Day by three deacons, on St. John's Day by three priests, and on Holy Innocents' Day by three boys. On the Feast of the Relics, after the processional respond was concluded, the relics were washed and an inventory of them read in English as the procession waited.

When the ceremonies at the rood were finished the procession moved on into the choir, singing another antiphon or respond. When the chant was over the priest terminated the procession with a versicle and prayer at the choir-step. (On ordinary Sundays the priest with his assistants then went into the canons' cemetery to sprinkle Holy Water and pray for the dead.)

Provisions were made for the bishop when he was present at these ceremonies:

> On any ordinary Sunday, if the Bishop should be the officiant, he shall normally enter the choir to bless the water dressed in a silk cope, with mitre and staff, and with the [usual] assistants. When the blessing of the salt and water is to be by the priest, as above, the bishop, specially vested, will withdraw to his episcopal throne, and there, after the aspersion of the main altar by the priest, sprinkle the canons as well as the rest of the clerks who shall come to him in the order already noted. [He shall] sing the versicle and prayer after the antiphon [of the aspersion], and after the return of the procession to the choir. Similarly on Sundays throughout the summer [it is] he [who] shall sing the versicle and prayer at the station before the rood (the priest, in processional dress shall say, as usual, the following prayers). After the return to the choir, while Tierce and Sext are being sung, [he shall] vest for Mass.
>
> If the bishop is not to be the celebrant, then in choir habit, with gloves and staff, he shall sprinkle the clerks as above; but walk with silk cope, mitre and staff always at the end of the procession. The hebdomadary priest shall carry out, as usual, everything pertaining to it.
>
> [On double feasts] if the bishop is present, all deacons and subdeacons will march together[1] in the procession.

This last direction is obscure. According to the Ordinal all the subdeacons and deacons assisted when the bishop said Mass. Most likely

---

[1] Ms: "processionaliter."

they marched in two groups in place of the single sub-deacon and single deacon of the ordinary procession.

The Special Processions

On six occasions the procession was exceptional.

On the feast of the Purification, after the blessing and distribution of the candles:

> The procession shall set out as on Christmas, [but] each clerk with a lighted candle. As well, after the thurifer, and before the sub-deacon, one of the altarists, in a surplice, shall carry a candle (blessed with the rest), which shall be specially reserved for use at the blessing of the font on the vigils of Easter and Pentecost. Three of the senior clerks, in silk copes, are to sing, together, the verse, in the *pulpitum*, facing the people.

On Palm Sunday, the blessing of the branches, and their distribution accompanied by antiphons, took place after the Asperges. Afterwards, constituted as on simple lenten Sundays:

> The procession shall go first through the west door [of the choir] and around the cloister, then through the Canons' Door to the place of the first station, on the north side of the church, at the extreme west end (at the Church of St. Mary of Sarum, before the cross in the north cemetery).

Here the Gospel *Cum appropinquasset Jesus Jerosolymis* of St. Matthew was read, and at the words, "Benedictus qui venit in nomine Domini," a second procession approached the first: in front a silver cross with crucifix, and two banners; then two clerks of the second rank, in choir habits, carrying a feretory (prepared during the distribution of the branches) containing the relics, and the consecrated Host in a pyx; one clerk holding a canopy over the feretory on one side, and another, in front, carrying a lighted lantern— both in surplices. What the bearers of the cross and banners in the second procession wore is not stated. On all other occasions, and probably here, they were vested in albs with amices.

When the Gospel was finished, three clerks of the second rank, in choir habits, left the procession, and on the west side of the relics, in front of the cemetery cross, facing the people, began a hymn. The first verse sung, the two processions combined; but the cross of the first procession, which was plain, without crucifix, was taken away by the acolyte. After the hymn was finished, the procession advanced to the place of the second station:

16

the feretory with the reliquary, together with the lighted lantern and all the ministers previously mentioned, between the sub-deacon and the thurifer, with banners on each side.

This second station was held on the south side of the church, where seven boys, from a raised position, sang a hymn.   When this was finished, the procession continued:

through the cloister, along the right-hand side, [out the *porta canonicorum*?] to the western door of the church.

Here, three clerks of the higher rank, in choir habits, facing the people, sang the verse of the processional antiphon; after which the procession moved on to the last station:

They are to enter the church through this same door, under the feretory and reliquary raised across it.

This fourth station was before the uncovered[1] rood, in the church.   Here an antiphon was sung; this finished, the procession entered the choir, where it terminated in the usual way, the priest singing a versicle and prayer.

On Ascension Thursday the procession was made up as on other double feasts, except that: (a) banners were carried, as in the rogation procession the previous day (see below), (b) a reliquary was carried after the thurible by two junior clerks in silk copes. The route was quite different:

The procession shall go down the middle of the choir and church, and out the west door; around the outside of the entire church and atrium; around the cloister, entering by the door next to the canons' cemetery [out the *porta canonicorum*?]; back into the church by the same door through which it left, to the rood.

It terminated as usual. On Corpus Christi, the procession was similar to that on Ascension, except that the priest carried the Blessed Sacrament. Over it, clerks in surplices carried a silk covering on four poles, and on each side, lighted candles.

Chambers, Henderson, Frere and Harrison believed that the Easter procession—and consequently Pentecost's, which was to be the same— was just as on ordinary double feasts. In fact, the route of the procession on these days was like that on Palm Sunday, Ascension, and Corpus Christi. The opening of the Processional's directions for Easter is ambiguous: "... the procession shall go down the middle of the choir and church, circling the church and cloister." However, the closing words of

[1] Images were normally veiled in Lent.

the rubric direct that the procession should then return "to the cross *in the church* through the same door *by which it left* (usque ad crucem in ecclesiam per idem ostium quo egressa est)." It was intended for the procession to go around the *outside* of the church and cloister, and this is made perfectly clear in one of the manuscripts of the Processional (Ms Bodley 637, folio 85v) by the addition of a single word to the first part of the Easter rubric translated above: "et exeat processio per medium chori et ecclesiae *extrinsecus* circumeundo ecclesiam et claustrum."

Processions were also held:

a. After Vespers, on the eve of the feast of any saint with an altar in the church:

> After all memorials, there is to be a procession to the altar of the saint, with taperers, thurifer, and a boy carrying the book in front of the priest, without a cross; the choir are to follow in ordinary habits, singing the respond.
> During the singing of the verse, the priest shall cense the altar, and the image [of the saint] if there is one, and afterwards sing a versicle and prayer.

The procession terminated in the choir in the usual manner.

According to the Ordinal the procession left the choir by the south door, and returned by the west. The priest and his ministers were probably dressed as in the Vespers processions on Saturdays throughout the summer: the taperers and thurifer in albs, the boy in a surplice, the priest in a surplice and silk cope. The choir rulers would be dressed as usual in surplices and silk copes and would walk after the priest.

Similar processions, in honour of St. Stephen, St. John, the Holy Innocents, and St. Thomas of Canterbury, were held in Christmas Week, but with the greater solemnity, and certain special ceremonies, of the Christmas season:

> On Christmas Day, after vespers, after the singing of the first *Benedicamus*, all the deacons are to assemble in silk copes and carrying lighted candles in their hands. The procession, singing the respond, will go down the middle of the choir to the altar of St. Stephen. Three deacons shall sing the verse; all the deacons together shall sing the prose. The chorus [vocalizing on the final vowel] or the organ shall answer with the melody of the prose after each verse. During the singing of the prose, the priest is to cense, first the altar, and then the image of St. Stephen; and afterwards, in a medium voice, sing the versicle and prayer.

The ordinal gives a more detailed description. We read that the procession was to leave the choir by the south door, and, re-entering by the west door, proceed up the middle of the choir and out the north door, to the altar. The verger (omitted in the Processional description) was to be a clerk in a surplice. The boy in front of the priest carried a book with a light. After the return to the choir through the west door, the chorus were to stand in front to the boys' benches during the concluding prayer; and this finished, the final *Dominus vobiscum* and *Benedicamus Domino* of Vespers were sung.

On the following evening a similar procession, substituting the priests for the deacons, was made to the Apostles' Altar.

On St. John's Day, substituting the boys, and the boy bishop for the officiant, it was made to the Altar of the Holy Trinity and All Saints[1] (called the *Salve*), and afterwards:

> Let them enter the choir through the west door, as above, and all the boys withdraw to the higher rank of seats on both sides of the choir; then the boy bishop, in a medium voice, from his seat, shall sing the versicle and prayer.

Canons were to serve at the disposition of the boys as ministers in this procession, the greater carrying the thurible and the book, and the lesser, the candles.

On the eve of the feast of St. Thomas, the normal procession to the saint's altar was given the distinction of a prose, sung, in surplices, by "all who wished."

b. On Ash Wednesday, after Sext, and after the sermon to the people:

> The priest of the highest dignity —in a red silk cope and other priests' vestments —with a deacon on his right, and a sub-deacon on his left, and the other ministers of the altar [i.e. two taperers, and two thurifers] — who are all to be in albs and amices —shall proceed to the vestibule to the altar step, preceded by a hair-cloth banner.

The bearer of the banner was doubtless vested like the others in alb and amice.

At the altar step, the penitential psalms were said in prostration, and the ashes blessed. After the distribution of the ashes, the priest sang a versicle and two prayers.

> These finished, the procession shall set off down the middle of the choir to the western door of the church, with taperers and thurifers, without a cross, a hair-cloth banner in front, those of greater dignity first.

[1] There was no altar of St. John the Apostle nor of the Holy Innocents at Sarum.

Then the officiant shall cast out, one by one, the penitents, with the help of one of the choir priests leading them to him by the right hand (should the bishop be present, the arch-deacon shall assist him); kissing the hand of the officiant, the penitents are to go out. Meanwhile, responds shall be sung.

After the penitents have been ejected, let the door of the church be closed, and the procession return to the choir in the usual manner, the banner left against the wall on the left side of the presbytery, on no account to be removed from there until the procession on Maundy Thursday. Neither versicle nor prayer is said; but the Introit of the Mass is intoned at once.

c. On all Wednesdays and Fridays of Lent, except on feasts of nine lections, after None:

The procession, without a cross, shall set out through the north door of the presbytery, to one of the altars on that side, the priest with his assistants [i.e. two taperers, a thurifer, sub-deacon and deacon], all dressed in albs and amices, the chorus following, in choir habits, singing one of the specified responds. After the respond, the clerks shall perform the prostration, in the same order as they are disposed in the procession. After the candles are set upon the altar, the priest, with the deacon on the right and the sub-deacon on the left, shall make his prostration at the altar step.

When the procession is to be to some altar on the south side, it is to go out through the south door of the presbytery; and when to some altar on the west side of the choir, then through the west door —for the processions hall not always be to the one altar, but, according to the regulations, to all the altars.

The procession returned to the choir, always by the west door. As on Ash Wednesday, Mass was begun immediately.

d. On Maundy Thursday:

None sung, the procession shall proceed as on Ash Wednesday: the priest of highest dignity in priests' vestments and a red silk cope, with two deacons in albs and amices, but without a sub-deacon, and without a cross, a hair-cloth banner [carried by an acolyte in alb and amice][1] in front, down the middle of the choir and through the west door of the church. Let there be present in the atrium those who are to be reconciled.

If the bishop assists, he shall wear his pontificals; and then the principal arch-deacon, on the part of the penitents, outside the door of the church, in a silk cope, shall read an address (which is not to be read when the bishop is absent).

When the address is finished, the officiant,[2] within the above door-way,

[1] Ms 148 of the Cathedral.
[2] Ms: "episcopus."

facing north, shall make a sign with his right hand to the penitents, as though to beckon them. The penitents are led by the hand, by some presbyter of the choir in ordinary habit, to the officiant; and by him restored to the bosom of the Church.

All of which finished, the procession shall return to the choir in the usual way.

This reconciliation ceremony was carried out to the singing of a psalm with its antiphon, begun by the officiant. Afterwards the penitential psalms were sung in choir.

After the mid-day meal, the water was blessed as on Sundays, but privately before the altar in the vestibule; then,

two of the priests of the highest dignity, with a deacon and sub-deacon of the second rank, and taperers of the first rank—all in albs without parures, and amices—with two clerks carrying wine and water (the bishop, when present, [with] mitre and staff),

proceeded, with the choir, to the main altar (and similarly, to each altar), which was washed, and left stripped until Holy Saturday. Before each altar, the choir sang a respond, and the more important of the two priests, a versicle and prayer. When they had finished, they entered the chapter house.

e. On Good Friday, after the cross had been unveiled by two senior priests, the choir sang a psalm, with its antiphon; then, while a hymn was sung, beginning with the most senior, the clerks and boys proceeded, unshod, to the adoration at the choir step. After the clergy had made their adoration, they sang an antiphon, seated in choir, while the ceremonies continued:

Let the cross be carried solemnly down the middle of the choir by the above two priests, taperers preceding [all unshod, in albs without parures], to some altar where it can be seen and adored by the people.

Returning to the vestibule while the above antiphon is being sung, let the taperers precede, to the High Altar, a priest (in a surplice, unshod, and without amice), carrying the Body of Christ in a pyx.

After the adoration is concluded, and the above antiphon with its verse, let the previous two priests, with the same reverence with which they had brought it, return the cross to the High Altar.

f. On Holy Saturday:

After None, the officiant, in priests' vestments with a red silk cope, the deacon in a dalmatic, the sub-deacon in a tunicle, and the rest of the ministers of the altar in albs and amices (without a light on the candles, or cross, or fire in the thurible), and an acolyte, someone of the first rank in a surplice, carrying, on a [candle] stick, an unlighted candle (made of three candles twisted together at the bottom, but separate at the top), shall go in procession, after the bearer of the Holy Water, who shall be dressed [in a surplice], the chorus following in ordinary habits, those of highest dignity first, down the middle of the choir to the column, in the south end of the church, near the font. [Here] the priest shall bless the fire, struck there between two columns. As they go, the whole choir shall recite a psalm, antiphonally, and without singing.

The priest is to stand next to the flame, facing east; on his left, the deacon, the sub-deacon to the left of the deacon; opposite the priest, a taperer, to whose right a boy [in a surplice] carrying the book; close behind the priest, the other taperer, at whose right, near the priest, the bearer of the Water; lastly, beyond all, on the west side, the bearer of the [candle] stick with the candle. The thurifer is to stand on the other side of the fire (viz, to the south) in order to receive it in the thurible after the blessing. All the ministers are to face the priest. The choir is to stand close by, on the north side.

After [their] blessing, some of the embers and incense are to be put in the thurible, and the new fire censed. Then the candle on the [candle] stick will alone be lighted from the new fire (the other lights in the church having been previously extinguished); and the procession shall return in the usual way to the choir.

During the return to the choir, two clerks of the second rank in surplices, walking behind the priest, sang a hymn; the chorus answered each verse with the refrain.

After the blessing of the Paschal candle, and the singing of the seven-fold litany, five deacons of the second rank, in surplices, began the five-fold litany, sung in choir up to the utterance, "Sancta Maria," at which the procession set out:

First an acolyte carrying a cross, in alb and tunicle; then two taperers in albs and amices; next the thurifer, similarly dressed; then two boys in surplices, walking side by side, and on carrying the book, and on his right, the other, the candle for blessing the font; next, two deacons of the second rank, in albs and amices, walking together, one carrying the oil, and on his right, the other, the chrism; then the sub-deacon, in a tunicle; [next the deacon, in a dalmatic;] then the priest, in a red silk cope, the choir following in ordinary habits, the above [five] deacons in the midst of the clerks of the second rank, after the officiant. And going down the south aisle, they shall come to the font.

While the litany is being sung through to the end, the priest shall stand at the font-step, on the west side, and behind him, the five deacons singing the litany; at the other font-step: the boy carrying the book; then the deacon; then the sub-deacon; then the oil and chrism; then the bearer of the candle for the font; then the thurifer; and last, the acolyte carrying the cross —all facing east.

When the litany has ended, the officiant, facing east, shall be assisted in blessing the font by the ministers ranged around it: on the right, next to the priest, the deacon, the sub-deacon on the left; he who carries the chrism, next to the deacon, and he who carries the oil, next to the sub-deacon; opposite the priest, facing him, he who carries the cross; beside whom, similarly, the two taperers; and after the taperers, the thurifer; he who carries the candle, between the deacon and the chrism; the boy carrying the book, between the oil and the sub-deacon. The bishop, if present, shall occupy, as in all other processions, the last place behind the singers of the litany.

For the return to the choir, three clerks of the higher rank, in silk copes (two in red, and one in white), sang a litany, the first verse before the procession started back.

g. On Easter Day:

Before Matins, and before the ringing of the bells, the clerks are to gather at the church, and every light in the church lit. Two of the presbyters of the highest dignity, in surplices, with taperers and thurifers [in albs], shall come up to the sepulchre (the clergy standing around), and having first censed it —genuflecting with great veneration immediately after the censing—they shall place the Lord's Body, separately, upon the altar. While taking the cross from the sepulchre, the senior [priest] shall begin the first antiphon, with which the procession is to go through the south door of the presbytery, returning up the middle of the choir, with the cross from the sepulchre carried reverently between the above two priests on their arms, thurifers and taperers preceding, to one of the altars on the north side, the choir following in ordinary habits, those of highest dignity first.

The Lord's Body, in a pyx, left on the altar, in the care of the sub-treasurer, he shall at once hang it (in the pyx) in the tabernacle; and then all the bells are to be rung together.[1]

After the above antiphon and its verse have been concluded by the whole choir, let the person of highest dignity say the versicle and prayer at the station before the altar. The prayer fiinished, those of highest dignity first, all shall joyfully genuflect there, and adore the cross; and one by one, without procession, enter the choir.

At Vespers, there is to be a procession to the font, through the south door of the presbytery, with cross, taperers, and thurifer; then the oil and chrism carried by two deacons of the second rank —[all] dressed in albs; then the officiant in a [surplice[2] and a] red silk cope, after whom the secondary rulers; then the principal rulers.

The antiphon and first verse of the psalm which accompanied the procession were sung in the choir. At the font, the procession was disposed as follows:

First the cross bearer, then the taperers, then the thurifer, then the oil and chrism, then the secondary rulers, then three boys [in surplices]

[1] "In classicum."
[2] Ordinal.

singing [an Alleluia and its verse]; then, at the east step of the font, the boy carrying the book, and at the west step, the officiant, after whom the principal rulers.

After the boys had finished singing, the font was censed:

At the censing, the thurifer is to come up to the priest, and when it is done, return to his place; similarly, at the singing of the versicle and prayer, the taperers are to come up to the priest, and the boy holding the book, and after the prayer has been sung, return to their places. (The same order will be [observed] consequently, at the station before the cross, except that the secondary rulers and the three boys who had sung the *alleluia* shall stand next to the priest. At the end of the psalm, the priest shall go in front of the cross bearer, to cense the Crucifix, which done, he shall return to his place where he shall sing the versicle and prayer of the Cross.)

The procession moved to this station at the Rood singing another psalm with its antiphon. Afterwards, the procession terminated as usual, in the choir, where the ministers carrying the thurible, oil, and chrism immediately withdrew, and the priest concluded with another versicle and prayer.

h. On the six days following Easter, at Matins, after the first *Benedicamus*:

The procession shall be down the middle of the choir, to the Crucifix, with cross, taperers, and thurifer, singing the antiphon (on Thursday, Friday, and Saturday, without verse). On the [first]day, the verse shall be sung by two of the higher rank, in surplices, facing the clerks, in front of the entrance to the choir, but on the following [two] days, by two clerks of the second rank, in the above dress and position.

According to the Ordinal, the cross was carried by an acolyte in a surplice; a boy in a surplice carried the book for the priest; the taperers and thurifer wore albs, the priest an alb and cope. After the antiphon (and verse, when it was sung), the crucifix was censed, and a versicle and prayer sung, by the priest. The procession terminated in the choir, in the usual manner.

On the five days following Easter, at Vespers, there were processions to the font, similar to that of Easter, except that the Alleluia was omitted. On the Saturday following Easter, and on all Saturdays until the Ascension, except the feast of the Discovery of the Cross (should it fall on a Saturday), there was a procession at Vespers, similar to that at Matins of Easter Week, but without a cross. On the Saturday following Easter, and when a double feast was celebrated, the choir wore surplices; otherwise, their black copes (as usual). On the Saturday following Easter, whenever a double feast fell on a Saturday or Sunday, and on the last Saturday before

Ascension, the verse of the processional antiphon was sung at the entrance to the choir, by two clerks of the higher rank (in surplices), facing the people; otherwise, by two clerks of the second rank, facing the clergy.

i. On Rogation Monday, after None, there was a procession, constituted as on ordinary Sundays, except that: (1) the boy carrying the water wore his black cope, (2) a reliquary was carried after the thurible, by two sub-deacons of the second rank in choir habits, (3) the priest did not wear a silk cope, (4) banners were carried (doubtless by clerks in ordinary habits), the Dragon preceded by three red banners, at the head of the procession, the Lion second, and (any) others third.

> Let the procession go out, down the middle of the choir and church, through the west door of the church and the north portal of the enclosure,[1] to some church in the city.

The first antiphon was sung by the choir in the stalls, before the procession set out.

> The procession shall go directly into the church where the station is to be. When the antiphon or respond is finished, the priest shall sing the versicle and prayer of the saint whose church it is; after which follow the prayers said in prostration. These done, let Mass begin.
> As soon as Mass is finished, two clerks of the second rank (three clerks of the higher rank, if a double feast should occur that day), in the midst of the procession, in choir habits, shall sing the litany (up to the utterance, "Sancta Maria", before the procession sets out), [while] the procession returns, through the east door of the enclosure[2] and the door of the canons' cemetery, entering the choir through the west door. When the litany is finished, the priest, at the choir-step, shall sing the versicle and prayer.

On Rogation Tuesday, and Wednesday, after None, the procession was similar, except that on the vigil of the Ascension, the Dragon was put back to a position in front of the cross. The Consuetudinary directs, doubtless for Salisbury only, that on Rogation Monday the procession should pass through the west gate to the city, circle the town on the north side to the stational church and return by the east gate; on Tuesday the route is: east gate, south side of city, return by the west gate. No route is specified for the third Rogation Day.

---

[1] Ms: "Claustri," but doubtless the gate of the cathedral enclosure.
[2] Again, "Claustri."

j. On St. Mark's Day, when it fell on a ferial after the Octave of Easter, a procession similar to that on the Rogation Days, but without the Lion and Dragon, was made, after None, to some church in the city or suburbs.

k. At any time, in the face of some emergency, a procession, after None, and similar to that on St. Mark's Day, was made *causa necessitatis* to some altar in the church, or as above, to some church in the city or suburbs.

l. On the vigil of Pentecost, after None, the Easter vigil procession to the font was repeated.

m. On all Saturdays from Trinity Sunday to Advent, except double feasts, and on the eve of the feasts of the Discovery and Exaltation of the Cross (but never at Second Vespers of these two feasts), at Vespers, after all memorials, there was a procession to the rood, similar to that on the Saturday after Easter, except that the choir wore ordinary habits. When the Feast of the Discovery of the Cross happened to fall on Ascension the procession was held after Second Vespers, and with a processional cross.

n. For the reception of an archbishop, their own bishop, legate, cardinal, king, or queen, the procession, constituted as on a principal double feast, went down the middle of the choir and church, and out the west door to the place where the visitor was to be met. Here he was censed, sprinkled with Holy Water, and received by the two people of highest dignity in silk copes. The procession then returned as it had come, to the choir, where at the altar-step the Prayers in Prostration were sung.

III. THE CHANTS AND PRAYERS

The constitution and route of the processions—the subjects of the previous chapter—varied according to the importance, the festive or penitential character, or the special nature of the occasion. The chants which accompanied them, and the prayers sung at the stations and at the conclusion in the choir made the processions appropriate to the day or to the season of their occurrence.

Most of the antiphons, responds, versicles and prayers were taken from other services, and borrowed in a meaningful orderly way designed to make the processions a part of the Daily Office and more than mere adjuncts to the Liturgy. The sources of this material and the system which governed its choice are set out in this chapter. All of the borrowed chants are included and readily available in the published facsimiles of the Sarum Gradual and Antiphoner.[1] All of the processional prayers can be found in the Sarum Breviary.[2] Those chants which were special to the processions, or at least not used for any other purpose at Sarum, are included in full, transcribed here from the main source, Ms Rawl. lit. d. 4. In the account which follows three stages of the ceremonies are distinguished: (I) the procession from the choir, (II) the service at the station, and (III) the return. The chants and prayers chosen often gave these stages a contrasting liturgical character.

THE ORDINARY PROCESSIONS BEFORE THE HIGH MASS

I. The Procession from the Choir

Special chants were sung on the four Sundays of Advent; on Septuagesima and on all Sundays until Pentecost except Passion Sunday and the

---

[1] *Graduale Sarisburiense* (London, 1894), *Antiphonale Sarisburiense* (London, 1901-1925), both edited by W. H. Frere.

[2] The Sarum Breviary has been published (in the version of the earliest printed text) by Proctor and Wordsworth (in 3 vols., Cambridge, 1879-1886).

Sunday after Ascension; and on the feasts of Purification, Ascension, Corpus Christi, and the Dedication.

At the remaining processions, and sometimes in addition to the special pieces on the occasions just mentioned, borrowed responds were sung. As a rule, the choice was the last respond of the day's Matins, or when there was an extra chant provided, the last and sixth respond; but there were exceptions:

Christmas	the third respond of Matins
St. Thomas the Martyr	the third Matins respond
Epiphany	the third and sixth Matins responds
Passion Sunday	the respond of First Vespers
Palm Sunday	the third and sixth Matins responds
Corpus Christi	the third respond of Matins.

For the Sunday processions between Trinity and Advent a choice was allowed of any of the Matins responds of Trinity Sunday, provided that the last respond was sung on the last Sunday.

At certain times of the year, i.e. between the Octave of Epiphany and Septuagesima, the Octave of Easter and Ascension, and between Trinity Sunday and Advent,[1] the dominical services were to be set aside when the date happened to be that of an important feast. In such events the usual choice of chant was the last respond of the feast's Matins. Again there were a few exceptions:

St. Agnes	the third Matins respond
St. Clement	the third Matins respond
St. Peter in Chains	the eighth Matins respond
St. Agatha	the last respond of the Common Matins for a Virgin.

Proses, the same ones provided by the service books for Matins,[2] were sung to the responds of the processions on Christmas and the feasts of St. Stephen, St. John, the Holy Innocents, and St. Thomas the Martyr.

Although they may not completely explain the exceptions, a few remarks may be to the point. When the last Matins respond was not the choice for the procession the piece that was sung was in some way

---

[1] Although the rubrics forbid it, the services (and processions) of the Advent Sundays were set aside in some places for the feasts of St. Andrew and St. Nicholas, and even for the Octave of Conception. See Bodley, Ms liturg. 408; Caius College, Ms 436.

[2] By the end of the thirteenth century the proses were sung at Matins only when they had not been sung in procession. See the directions in the Ordinal (edited by W. H. Frere in *The Use of Sarum*, Cambridge, 1901, II, 30).

distinguished. For Christmas and the Feast of St. Thomas, when proses played an important part in the processions, the chants used were the only Matins responds provided with them. On Palm Sunday, Passion Sunday, and for the feasts of St. Agnes, St. Peter in Chains, and St. Clement, the respond of the procession was sung not only at Matins but at First Vespers. For Epiphany and Corpus Christi the responds were probably chosen for their texts: those of the first feast recount the journey (i.e. procession) of the Magi; the respond for Corpus Christi closes, "et ambulavit in fortitudine cibi illius usque ad montem Dei" (and marched on the strength of this food right to God's abode). The case of St. Agatha seems to involve an oversight in the compilation of the processional, and is discussed later.

The responds of the summer "histories" seem never to have been used like the others. All processions at Sarum were in honour of an important occasion or in commemoration of one. Processions which used the summer responds would be neutral in character and out of keeping with the rest. As it was, the ordinary Sunday processions during the summer were in continuing commemoration of the Feast of the Holy Trinity. The choice of any of the nine responds was doubtless offered to avoid the weekly repetition of the same chant. It should be mentioned that in practice many of the dominical processions were displaced by services of the saints.

Following are the special processional chants, first, *Missus est Angelus*, the antiphon for the Sundays of Advent (Folio 4).

Ex. 2.

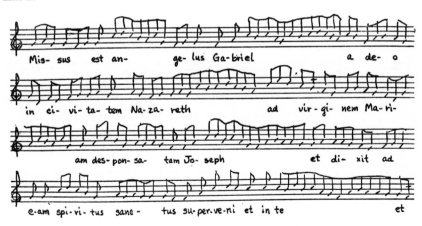

Ex. 2 (Continued).

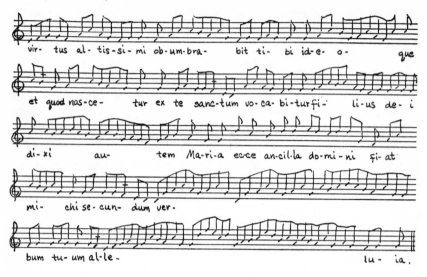

vir- tus al- tis-si- mi ob-um-bra- bit ti- bi id- e- o- que
et quod nas-ce- tur ex te sanc-tum vo-ca- bi-tur fi- li-us de- i
di- xi au- tem Ma-ri-a ec-ce an-cil-la do-mi- ni fi- at
mi- chi se- cun- dum ver-
bum tu- um al-le- lu - ia.

Ex. 3. *Ecce carissimi*, the antiphon for Septuagesima, Sexagesima and Quinquagesima Sundays (folio 21).

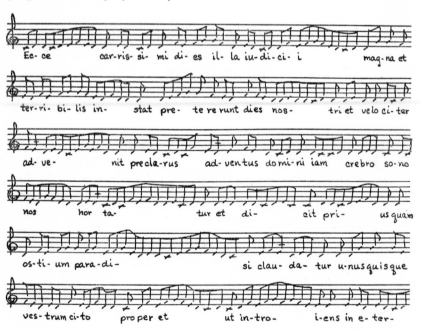

Ec- ce car-ris- si- mi di- es il- la iu-di-ci- i mag-na et
ter-ri- bi- lis in- stat pre- te re runt dies nos- tri et velo ci- ter
ad- ve- nit precla-rus ad-ventus do mi-ni iam crebro so-no
nos hor ta- tur et di- cit pri- us quam
os-ti- um para-di- si clau- da- tur u-nusquisque
ves-trum ci-to pro per et ut in-tro- i-ens in e- ter-

Ex. 3 (continued).

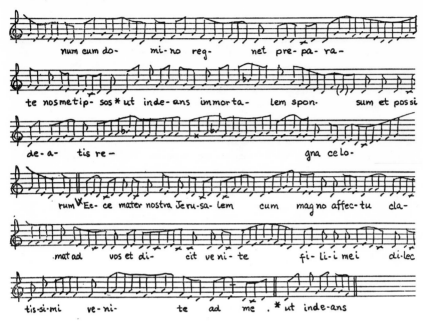

Ex. 4. *Cum venerimus*, the antiphon for the first two Sundays of Quadra-gesima (folio 31).

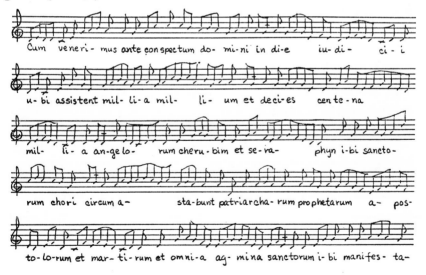

Ex. 4 (Continued)

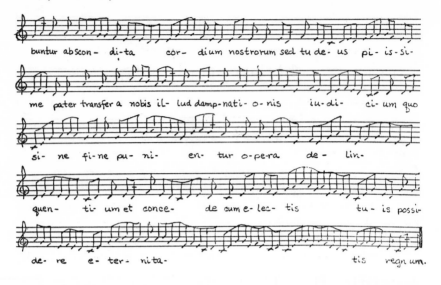

buntur abscon - di-ta cor- dium nostrorum sed tu de- us pi- is-si-

me pater transfer a nobis il- lud damp-nati- o- nis iu-di- ci- um quo

si- ne fi-ne pu- ni- en- tur o-pe-ra de - lin-

quen- ti- um et conce- de cum e- lec- tis tu - is possi-

de- re e- ter- ni-ta- tis regn um.

Ex. 5. *In die quando,* the antiphon for the third and fourth Sundays of Quadragesima (folio 36).

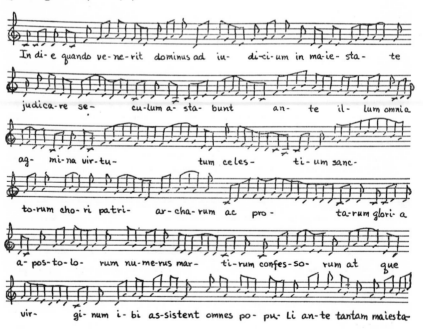

In di- e quando ve- ne-rit dominus ad iu- di-ci- um in ma-ie- sta- te

judica-re se- cu-lum a- sta- bunt an- te il- lum omnia

ag- mi-na vir-tu- tum ce les- ti- um sanc-

to-rum cho-ri patri- ar-cha-rum ac pro - ta-rum glori- a

a- pos-to-lo- rum nu-me-rus mar- ti-rum confes-so- rum at que

vir- gi- num i- bi as-sistent omnes po- pu- li an-te tantam maiesta-

Ex. 5 (continued).

tem domi-num nimi-um per-terri-ti dies il- la di-es

ir- ae dies tribulati o- nis di-es mise-ri e et vindic-te dies tu-

be et clango- ris dies nu-bis et ca-li- gi- nis dies il- la ni-mi-

um er-it im- pi- is a- ma- ra O quam fe-li-ces

e- runt il- li qui vo-cem domini me-ru-e- runt au-di- re ve-

ni- te bene-dic- ti patris mei per-ci-

pi-te reg- num quod vo- bis pre pa- ra-

tum est ab or- i- gi-.ne mun- di.

For Palm Sunday:

Ex. 6. The antiphon, *Prima autem azimorum* (folio 41v).

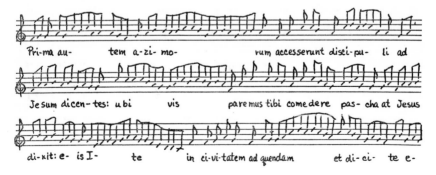

Pri-ma au- tem a-zi-mo- rum accesserunt disci-pu- li ad

Je sum dicen-tes: u bi vis pare mus tibi come de re pas- cha at Jesus

di-xit: e- is I- te in ci-vi-tatem ad quendam et di-ci- te e-

Ex. 6 (continued).

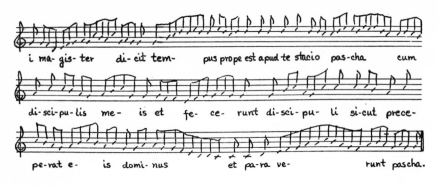

i ma- gis- ter   di- cit tem-   pus prope est apud te stacio pas-cha   cum

di-sci-pu-lis   me-   is et   fe- ce- runt di-sci- pu- li si-cut prece-

pe-rat e-   is domi- nus   et pa-ra ve-   runt pascha.

Ex. 7. The antiphon, *Cum appropinquaret* (folio 42).

Cum   appropin- quaret do-   mi- nus Je-ro- so-   li- mammi- sit

du-   os ex disci-pulis su-is   di- cens: I-   te in

cas-tellum quod est   con- tra   vos et in- ve-ni- e-   tis

pul-lum a- si-ne al-li-   ga- tum   su-per quem nullus ho-

mi num se-dit solvi-   te et ad- du-   ci-te mi- chi si

quis nos   in-ter-ro- ga- ve-   rit di-   ci-te o-pus

do-   mi-   ni   est sol- len-   tes   ad-   duxe-runt ad Je- sum

34

Ex. 7 (continued).

et im-po-su e-runt il- li ves-ti-men-ta et sedit su-per e-um

a- li- i propter- ne-bant vesti-menta su-a in vi - a

a- li- i ramos de ar-bo-ri-bus ex-ter - ne-bant et qui se-que-

ban-tur cla-ma-bant O-san-na be ne-dictus qui ve-nit in no-mi-ne domi-

ni be-ne-dic- tum regnum patris nos-tri Da- vid O-san- na in ex-

cel- sis mise-re-re no- bis fi- li Da- vid.

Ex. 8. The antiphon, *Cum audisset* (folio 43).

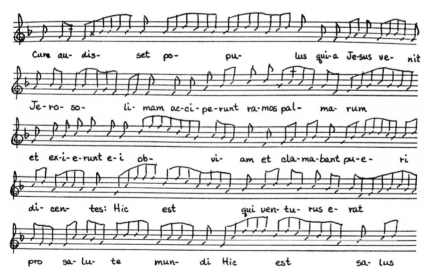

Cum au-dis- set po- pu- lus qui-a Je-sus ve- nit

Je-ro- so- li- mam ac-ci-pe-runt ra-mos pal- ma- rum

et ex-i-e-runt e-i ob- vi- am et cla-ma-bant pu-e- ri

di- cen- tes: Hic est qui ven-tu- rus e- rat

pro sa-lu- te mun- di Hic est sa- lus

Ex. 8 (continued).

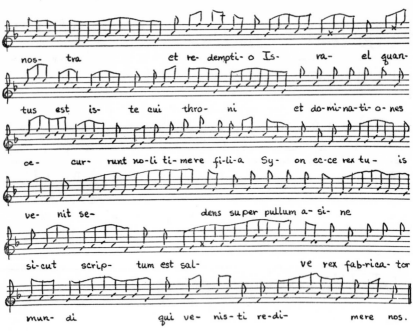

Ex. 9. The antiphon, *Ante sex dies sollennitatis* (folio 43v).

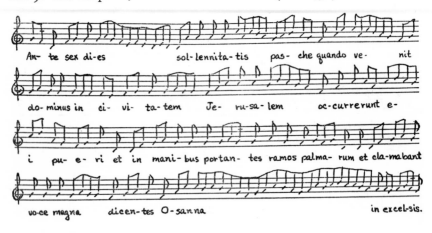

Ex. 10. The antiphon, *Ante sex dies passionis* (folio 44).

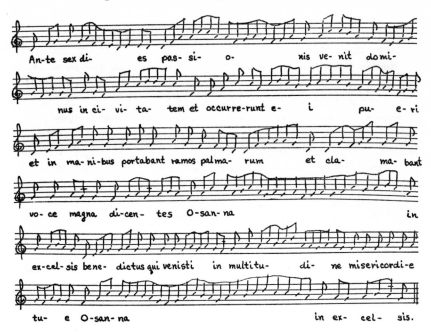

Ex. 11. The hymn, *En rex venit* (folio 45).

Ex. 11 (continued).

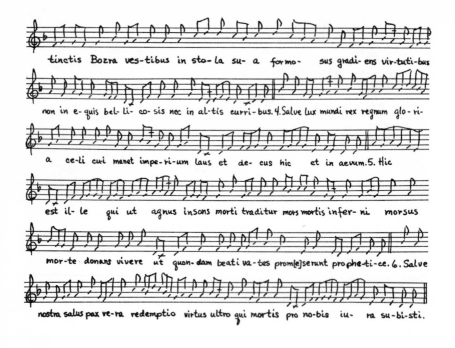

tinctis Bozra ves-ti-bus in sto-la su-a formo- sus gradi-ens vir-tuti-bus
non in e-quis bel-li- co-sis nec in al-tis curri-bus. 4. Salve lux mundi rex regnum glo-ri-
a ce-li cui manet impe-ri-um laus et de- cus hic et in aevum. 5. Hic
est il-le qui ut agnus insons morti traditur mors mortis infer- ni morsus
mor-te donans vivere ut quon-dam beati va-tes prom[e]serunt prophe-ti-ce. 6. Salve
nostra salus pax ve-ra redemptio virtus ultro qui mortis pro no-bis iu- ra su-bi-sti.

Ex. 12. The antiphon, *Occurunt turbae* (folio 46v).

Oc-cur-runt tur-be cum flori-bus et pal-mis redemptori ob- vi- am
et vic-to-ri trium-phanti dignadant obse-qui-a fi-li- o de- i a-re-gen-
tes praedicant et in laudem Christi vo- ces to-nant per nubi-la Ho-san- na.

Ex. 13. The respond, *Collegerunt pontifices* (folio 48).

Ex. 14. The antiphon, *Ave rex noster* (folio 49).

For Easter, the hymn *Salve festa dies* (... qua deus infernum) (folio 87).

Ex. 15.

This same hymn, with different texts to suit the occasions, was sung for the processions on several other feasts:

Pentecost — *Salve festa dies ... qua nova de celo*
Ascension — *Salve festa dies ... qua deus in celum*
Corpus Christi — *Salve festa dies ... qua caro Messiae*
Dedication — *Salve festa dies ... qua sponso sponsa*
Holy Name — *Salve festa dies ... qua Jesus.*

The texts can be found in the *Graduale Sarisburiense*.

For the Sunday following Easter, the antiphon *Sedit Angelus* (folio 88v).

Ex. 16.

For the Sunday following the Octave of Easter and for all Sundays until Ascension the antiphon *Ego sum alpha* (folio 94).

Ex. 17.

E- go sum al- pha et O pri- mus et no- vis-si- mus in- i- ti- um

et fi- nis qui an- te mundi princi- pi- um et in se-cu- lum se-cu-

li vi- vo in e- ternum ma- nus me- e que vos

fe- ce-runt cla- vis con- fi- xe- runt propter nos fla-gel- lis

Je- sus sum spi- nis co- ro- na-tus sum a- quam pe-

ti- i pen- dens et a-ce- tum po re- xe-runt in escam me-am

fel de- de-runt et in la- tus lan-ce- am mortuus et se- pul-

tus resurrexi vo- bis-eum sum vi-de-te quia ego ip- se sum et non

est de-us preter- me alle- lu-ia. ℣ Ego sum vestra re-dem-ci-o ego sum rex vester

Ego vos re-sus- ci- ta- bo in di- e no- vis-si- mo. vi-de- te

For Purification:

Ex. 18. The antiphon, *Ave gratia plena* (folio 139v).

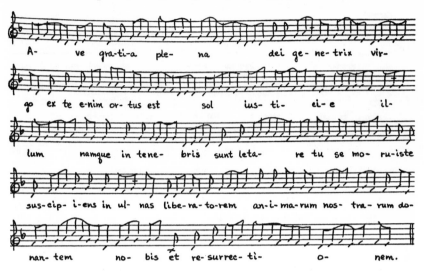

Ex. 19. The antiphon, *Adorna thalamum* (folio 140).

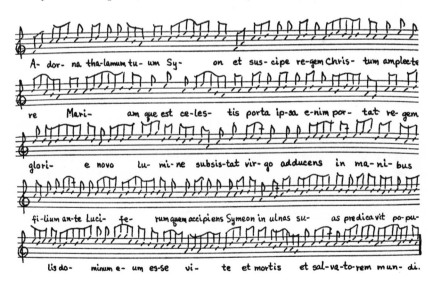

II. *The Station*

On ordinary Sundays, except in parochial churches, it was the custom to say the Bidding Prayers during the procession, at the Rood step, just before the return to the choir.[1] In the period from Trinity Sunday to Advent these prayers were preceded by a general commemoration of the Holy Cross consisting of an antiphon, versicle, and prayer. There was a choice of either of the antiphons of the second and third psalms of the second nocturne of the Feast of the Exaltation of the Cross. The prayer is one of those provided for the memorial of the Cross at Matins during this period; the versicle is one which occurs frequently in the Offices of the feasts of the Discovery and Exaltation of the Cross.

III. *The Return to the Choir*

On the most important feasts[2] and Sundays[3] the pieces sung in the last

---

[1] These prayers, mainly in English, were for living and dead prelates, rulers, patrons, etc., and were normally said at Mass, as today, after the Gospel. For a discussion of the Bidding of the Bedes see F. E. Brightman, *The English Rite* (London, 1915) II, 1020 ff.

[2] Principal and major doubles.

[3] Greater Sundays of the first and second class.

stage of the procession were specially appropriate to the day—*de festo*, in the words of the rubrics. On lesser occasions the chant, versicle and prayer formed a commemoration appropriate to the season.

The rubrics require that for the procession on Conception the service of the Nativity is to be used, only changing "nativitas" to "conceptio" wherever necessary. If this direction were followed to the letter, Conception, a minor double, received a procession like those on the greatest feasts. This discrepancy has been corrected in two of the Processionals, Bodley Ms liturg. 408 and Caius College Ms 436, where for the last stage of the procession an antiphon, versicle and prayer of All Saints are provided. At Sarum itself, however, the Return *de festo* was tolerated, perhaps as an extra dignity for a feast of Mary the patron saint: Ms 148 of the Cathedral specifies the Nativity versicle and prayer. Further discrepancies of this sort arose with the late additions to the Processional, but these will be discussed later.

The practice for the octaves of great feasts was not perfectly consistent with the rule. The celebration of the octave was less solemn than that of the feast itself, and this is reflected in the processions.[1] If there had been a prose or an extra chant it was omitted. Similarly, in keeping with the lower rank of the octave, the concluding chant, versicle and prayer were usually not those of the procession on the feast, but formed an appropriate general commemoration. For the octaves of Christmas, Epiphany, and Ascension, however, the pieces sung in the last stage of the procession were just as on the feast itself.

When the Return was *de festo*

In most of the processions on these occasions the chant sung while the clergy entered the choir was the last respond of Matins. When this chant had already been used, and in a few cases even though it had not, the choice was as follows:

the sixth Matins respond	Trinity, Purification
the respond of Vespers	Palm Sunday, Dedication, Ascension
the Magnificat antiphon	Christmas, Corpus Christi, Nativity, All Saints.

For Easter all the processional chants were special.

There seems to be no rule which would explain all these choices.

---

[1] There would be a procession, of course, only on the Sunday within the octave.

Where the last Matins respond has been avoided, as for Christmas, Purification, Corpus Christi, and Dedication, its text, in each case, is vague or general in character. The text of the piece chosen exactly epitomizes the occasion. In any case, for the processions on the greatest feasts it may be that the choice of chants was prescribed by a widespread tradition which superseded local considerations.

The versicle sung at the conclusion of the procession was usually that of Lauds. There were three exceptions. For Assumption, Nativity, and the Feast of All Saints the versicle of First Vespers was sung. The Lauds versicle for Assumption and Nativity happen to be the same; the use of the Vespers versicle in these cases may have been to avoid such a correspondence. *Letamini in domino*, used on All Saints' Day, was sung regularly in processions which included a commemoration of All Saints, and was probably sung on this occasion out of habit. Other similar cases where *Letamini* is found in place of the expected versicle will be met later.

The closing prayer at the choir-step was the Collect of the Day's Mass, except on the Feast of Purification, when there was a special prayer.

On Lesser Occasions

In the remaining processions the pieces sung in the last stage constituted general commemorations of the Virgin, the Resurrection, and occasionally of All Saints.

During most of the year the commemorations were of the Virgin, the patroness of Sarum Cathedral. On Circumcision and in all processions until Purification, and in all processions not principally devoted to the Virgin from Trinity to Advent—except between Assumption and Nativity—any of the Marian Antiphons[1] might be sung. From the Octave of Assumption until Nativity, as a sort of remembrance of the first feast, there was a choice from four Assumption chants: the antiphons to the first, second, and fifth psalms and Magnificat of First Vespers. There was a similar observance for the Nativity. See, below, the provisions for the Feast of the Exaltation of the Cross.

On days of lower rank when the service was in honour of the Virgin, the pieces of the last stage of the processions were in commemoration of

---

[1] The Processional provides a collection of Marian Antiphons for various occasions. They are given with the pieces for the processions on Saturdays from Trinity to Advent, but they are referred to from other parts of the book. Six pieces are given; only one, *Beata Dei genetrix*, the antiphon to the fifth psalm at First Vespers of the Nativity, is used in the Office.

All Saints. (Only for the greatest feasts were all the pieces to be *de festo*.) The usual chant was the antiphon to the Magnificat of the Feast of All Saints, but when this happened to have been sung at a Vespers procession the previous evening the Benedictus antiphon was substituted.

From the Octave of Easter until Ascension in all processions except those for occasions of principal or major double rank there were commemorations of the Resurrection. There was a choice of two of the special Easter processional antiphons.

The versicle and prayer on these occasions were usually those of the corresponding current Matins memorial. The one outright exception is the use of *Letamini* instead of the memorial versicle in the commemorations of the Resurrection. There are two other apparent discrepancies wich require explanation. The Processionals provided for the Eastertide processions the versicle *Surrexit Dominus de sepulchro*, another versicle, *Surrexit Dominus vere*, or an ambiguous cue "Surrexit Dominus." Even though it is specified in only a few of the sources,[1] it is the second versicle, that of the Matins memorial of the Resurrection, which would appear to be correct, for this choice puts the Eastertide processions in accord with all the others. *Surrexit Dominus de sepulchro*, the versicle of the procession on Easter and its Octave, is probably a mis-reading of the cue.

The prayer sung in processions from Trinity to Advent is not listed in any of the Sarum books as a Matins memorial prayer. But a curious direction in the Breviary:[2]

> non dicitur oratio *Concede quaesumus misericors deus* ad memoriam sancta Maria nisi ad processionem tantum

implies, in specifically restricting its use to the processions, that it had been used previously in the Office. The York Breviary[3] does in fact list this prayer with those for the Matins (and Vespers) memorials of the Virgin. For the Feast of the Exaltation of the Cross, which fell within the Octave of the Nativity, the commemoration of the Virgin in the last stage of the procession took the form of a memorial of the Marian feast. The chant was *Beata dei genetrix*;[4] afterwards were sung the Nativity Lauds versicle and Mass Collect.

[1] Rawl. lit. e. 45, Jesus College Ms 62, St. John's Cambridge Ms 151, Ms 148 of Sarum Cathedral, British Museum add. 12194 (a Sarum Gradual of the early thirteenth century).
[2] *Ed. cit.*, II, col. 91.
[3] Published in 1880 as volume 71 of the publications of the Surtees Society, I, col. 940.
[4] See page 46, note 1.

For the return of the procession to the choir on Easter Sunday the antiphon, *Christus resurgens* (folio 86):

Ex. 21.

Christus re-sur- gens ex mor- tu- is iam non mo-ri-
tur mors il- li ul-tra non do-mi-na- bi- tur
quod e- nim vi- vit vi- vit de-o al- le-
lu-ia al- le-lu- ia ℣ Dicant nunc Iu-de- i quo
mo-do mi- li- tes custo-di-en- tes se- pul- chrum per-di-de-runt
re-gem ad la-pi-dis posissi- o- nem qua- re non ser-vabant pet- ram
iu- sti- ci- e aut se-pul- trum re-dant aut resurgen-tem a-
do- rant no-bis cum di- cen- tes: Al- le- lu- ia al- le- lu-ia.

THE PROCESSIONS AT VESPERS AND MATINS

I. *The Procession from the Choir and the Station*

Processions in Honour of the Saints

a. *The Vespers processions of Christmas Week.* The pieces sung in the first part of the procession formed a commemoration of the saint: the respond was the same one provided for his procession before Mass; the versicle and prayer were those of his Vespers memorial. Memorials of the saints were called for in this week in lieu of their displaced Vespers, and would have to be sung in choir if there were no procession. One other similar instance will be met later. In all other cases the memorials sung in the processions were not strictly necessary.

b. *The processions at First Vespers on the feasts of saints with altars in the church.* The Processional includes twelve of these, and a general rubric for any others. The pieces of the first part of the procession formed a commemoration of the saint whose altar it was. In six of the processions the chant sung on the way to the altar was the last respond of the saint's Matins, the same chant provided for his procession before Mass. In the remaining six the choice was as follows:

St. Margaret
St. Michael
St. Edward   the sixth respond of the saint's Matins
St. Edmund the Bishop
St. Kathrine
St. John the Baptist   the third Matins respond.

The use of the sixth respond in place of the last may have been to avoid the repetition of the same piece at Vespers and again in the procession the next morning. But why a similar substitution was not made in the other cases is not clear. The sixth respond of St. John the Baptist was probably avoided because of its prominent reference to St. Elizabeth. The usual correspondence with the Vespers memorials is not found in these processions, for the obvious reason that Office memorials did not occur for most of the saints involved. Those in the processions seem to have been made up especially for the occasions. A Matins memorial of St. Edward was sung on the Vigil of Epiphany, and a Vespers memorial of St. Andrew during the Octave of his feast, but these memorials are not the same as those sung in the processions; the versicles do not correspond.

For St. Andrew the versicle sung was that of the Common First Vespers of an Apostle; for St. John the Baptist and St. Lawrence, that of Common first Vespers of a Martyr; for St. Michael, the versicle of the first nocturne of his feast; for St. Mary Magdalen, the versicle of her Second Vespers; in the remaining seven processions, a versicle from the Common of the Saints, the ubiquitous *Ora pro nobis N.* (ut digni efficiamur promissionibus Christi).

The prayer at the altar was as follows:

St. Andrew   the Collect of the Mass of his feast, unless this had been sung at Vespers, in which case a prayer from the Common, *Quaesumus omnipotens Deus ut beatus N.*

St. Lawrence	the Collect of the Mass of his feast
St. Michael	the Postcommunion of the Mass of his feast
St. John the Baptist	the Collect of the Mass of the Feast of the Decollation of John the Baptist
Translation of St. Edward the King	the Mass Collect of the Feast of St. Edward the King (January 5)
St. Margaret	the Collect of the Common Mass for a virgin martyr
St. Edmund the King	the Collect of the Common Mass for a martyr.

For the processions of St. Nicholas, St. Edmund the Bishop, St. Martin, St. Mary Magdalen, and St. Kathrine there were special prayers.

The rationale for these choices is given in the rubric providing for any further Vespers processions to altars:

> When the prayer of the Vigil is said at First Vespers ..., then at the procession the prayer of the [feast] day shall be said; similarly, when the prayer of the feast [day] is said at First Vespers, then at the procession a prayer from the Common shall be said — unless there is a special one... as for the Feast of St. Nicholas and the like.

The general rubrics give no instructions for choosing the versicle sung at the altar or the chant sung on the way to it in any other processions.

Processions in Honour of the Cross

a. The pieces sung in the processions to the Rood at Matins in Easter Week (the Easter procession before Matins will be considered later) formed commemorations of the Cross and of the Virgin. The special Easter antiphon *Christus resurgens* was sung on the way to the rood; the versicle and prayer at the rood were those of the Matins memorial of the Cross in Paschal Time.

b. At Vespers on the five days following Easter the pieces sung in the first part of the processions formed commemorations of the Resurrection and the Cross. Two of the special Easter chants (*Sedit Angelus, Christus resurgens*) without their verses[1] accompanied the procession to the font and the return to the rood. The versicle of Easter Lauds and a special prayer for each night were sung at the font. The versicle and prayer at the rood were those of the memorial of the Cross at Vespers in Paschal Time.

For the Vespers procession of the Exaltation of the Cross the pieces sung in the first stage were originally the same as on the other feast. In the latest manuscripts (Rawl. lit. d. 4, Marsh Library Z4. 2. 20) and in the editions, the prayer was the Collect of the votive Mass of the Holy Cross.

[1] However, in Bodley Ms liturg. 408 the rubrics specify that the verses shall be sung.

II. *The Return to the Choir*

The pieces sung in the last stage of the processions were ordinarily in honour of the Virgin. There was usually a free choice of any of the Marian Antiphons plus, during Christmas Week, *Felix namque*, the third Matins respond of the Feast of the Nativity (of Mary). Specific Marian antiphons are sometimes prescribed. Between the Octave of the Assumption and Nativity, as a sort of remembrance of the first feast, Assumption pieces were sung, the same as in the dominical processions of the same period (see above). The versicle and prayer[1] were those of the current Vespers memorial of the Virgin or, in the case of the Matins processions, the Matins memorial. For the Vespers procession of the Exaltation of the Cross the final chant, versicle and prayer—the same as those in the procession the next morning before Mass—were in commemoration of the Nativity, within whose Octave this feast fell.

In Advent, within the octaves of Assumption and Nativity, or whenever there had been a memorial of the Virgin at Vespers just prior to the procession, the last stage was dedicated to All Saints. The chant was the Magnificat antiphon of the Feast of All Saints. The prayer was that of the current All Saints Vespers memorial. The versicle was always *Letamini in domino*, even in Advent, when it was not the versicle of the current memorial.

THE SPECIAL PROCESSIONS

I. *Lenten Ceremonies*

a. The procession on Ash Wednesday to the door of the church for the expulsion of the penitents was made in silence. During the ceremony two pieces were sung, the seventh and second ferial responds of Septuagesima (probably chosen for their texts, which refer to the expulsion from Eden); for the return to the choir, the third respond of the first Sunday of Quadragesima was the choice—once again, probably for its text (*Emendemus in melius*).

b. For the lenten ferial processions, a choice was offered of a special respond, the Quadragesima respond *Emendemus*, and the Matins responds of Ash Wednesday—all of penitential character. At the altar were said the *preces in prostratione*.[2] Litanies were recited during the return to the choir.

---

[1] The summer prayer was *Concede*; see above, p. 47.

[2] A set of penitential versicles, with Psalm L, and a prayer.

c. The procession for the reconciliation of the penitents of Holy Thursday, and the return to the choir, were made in silence. Psalm XXXIII was recited during the reconciliation ceremony.

II. *Easter Ceremonies*

a. The procession on Holy Saturday to the place where the new fire was to be blessed was made to the recitation of Psalm XXVI. A hymn accompanied the return to the choir.

b. Litanies were sung during the procession and the return to the choir at the blessing of the font.

c. For the procession to the sepulchre on Easter morning before Matins the special processional antiphon, *Christus resurgens*, was sung, with the versicle of Easter Lauds and the prayer of the Matins memorial of the Cross in Paschal Time. The return to the choir was in silence.

d. The procession to the font at Vespers was accompanied by Psalm CXII. At the font were sung *Alleluia* (verse: *Laudate pueri*), the Easter Lauds versicle and a special prayer. Psalm CXIII was sung on the way to the rood. The versicle and prayer said there, and the pieces sung during the return to the choir were the same as those of the processions at Vespers of the following days (discussed above).

III. *Rogation Processions*

For the processions on the Monday, Tuesday, and Wednesday before Ascension, of the Major Litany, and *causa necessitatis*, special antiphons were sung, and when necessary, the Penitential Psalms and a litany. As the procession passed through the stational church a respond was sung of the saint whose church it was, followed by his versicle and prayer, followed by the *preces in prostratione* and Mass. There was a litany provided for each day for the return to the home church. The final versicle and prayer of the processions of the Major Litany, and of the first two Rogation Days, were those of the memorial of All Saints at Matins from Easter to the Ascension; but for the procession *causa necessitatis* (which could be held at any time), and on the vigil of the Ascension (which is officially outside Paschal Time), the versicle and prayer of the Matins memorial of All Saints of the summer period were used.

Following are the antiphons which accompanied the rogation processions.

Ex. 22. *Exurge domine adiuva* (folio 95).

Ex-ur-ge do- mi- ne ad-iu-va   nos et li-bera   nos propter no men
tu- um al- le- lu- i-   a. Ps. Deus au- ri-bus

Ex. 23. *Surgite sancti* (folio 95v).

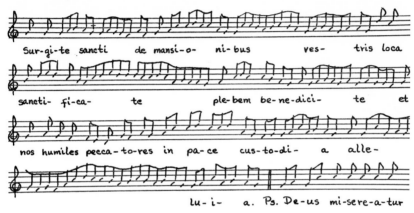

Sur-gi-te sancti   de mansi-o- ni-bus   ves-   tris loca
sancti- fi-ca-   te   ple-bem be-ne-dici-   te   et
nos humiles pecca-to-res in pa-ce cus-to-di-   a   alle-
lu- i-   a. Ps. De-us mi-se-re-a-tur

Ex. 24. *De Ierusalem exeunt* (folio 95v).

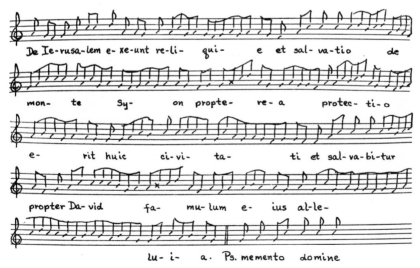

De Ie-rusa-lem e- xe-unt re-li-   qui-   e et sal- va-tio   de
mon-   te   Sy-   on propte-   re- a   protec- ti-o
e-   rit huic   ci- vi-   ta-   ti et sal-va-bi-tur
propter Da- vid   fa-   mu-lum e- ius al-le-
lu- i-   a. Ps. memento   domine

Ex. 25. *In nomine domini* (folio 96).

In no-mi-ne do-mi-ni de-i nos-tri ambu-la-bi- mus nos et om nes

po- pu- li quo-ni- am de Sy- on ex-hi- bit lex

et ver-bum do-mi- ni de Ie-ru- sa- lem regna-bit

do- mi- nus in e- ter- num al- le-

lu- ia. Ps. Le-ta-tus sum

Ex. 26. *Domine rex deus* (folio 96v).

Do-mi-ne rex de-us A-bra- ham dona no-bis plu-vi- am super

fa-ci- em ter- re ut dis- cat po-pu-lus is- te quia tu es

do- mi-nus de-us nos- ter al- le- lu-i- a. Ps. Exurgat deus

Ex. 27. *Numquid est in idolis* (folio 96v).

Numquid est in i- do-lis genti- um qui plu- at ni- si- tu de-

us aut celi pos- sunt da-re pluvi- am ni- si tu volu- e-

Ex. 27 (continued).

ris   tu   es do-mi-nus de-us nos-   ter quem expec-ta-

mus   do-na no- bis   plu vi- am al- le-

lu- i- a al-le-   lu- i- a. Ps. Sal-vum me

Ex. 28. *Exaudi domine populum* (folio 97).

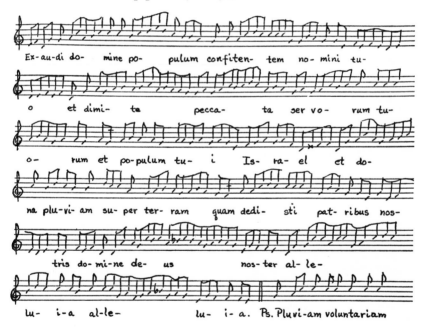

Ex-au-di do- mine po- pulum confiten- tem no- mini tu-

o   et dimi- ta   pecca- ta ser vo- rum tu-

o- rum et po-pulum tu- i Is- ra- el et do-

na plu-vi- am su- per ter- ram quam dedi- sti pat- ribus nos-

tris do- mi-ne de- us nos- ter al- le-

lu- i-a al-le- lu- i- a. Ps. Plu vi-am voluntariam

Ex. 29. *Respice domine* (folio 97v).

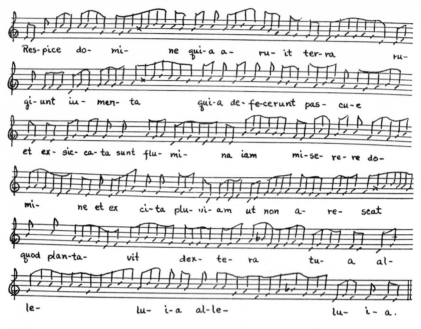

Res-pice do- mi- ne qui-a a- ru-it ter-ra ru-gi-unt iu-men-ta qui-a de-fe-cerunt pas-cu-e et ex-sic-ca-ta sunt flu-mi- na iam mi-se-re-re do-mi- ne et ex ci-ta plu-vi-am ut non a-re-scat quod plan-ta-vit dex-te-ra tu-a al-le- lu-i-a al-le-lu-i-a.

Ex. 30. *Inundaverunt aquae* (folio 98).

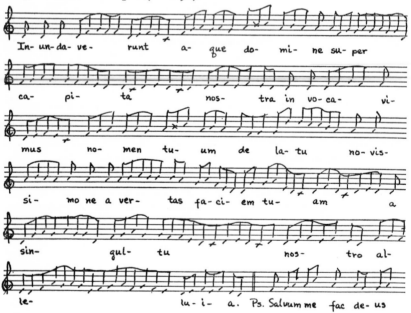

In-un-da-ve-runt a-que do-mi-ne su-per ca-pi-ta nos-tra in vo-ca-vi-mus no-men tu-um de la-tu no-vis-si-mo ne a ver-tas fa-ci-em tu-am a sin-gul-tu nos-tro al-le-lu-i-a. Ps. Salvum me fac de-us

Ex. 31. *Non nos demergat* (folio 98v).

Non nos de- mergat do- mi- ne tem- pes-tas a- que

ne- que ab- sor-be- at nos pro- fun- dum ne-

que ur- ge- at in nos pu- te-us os su- um mit-te

ma- num tu- am de al- to et li- be- ra nos

de a- quis mul- tis al- le- lu- i-a. Ps. Ex-au-di nos domine

Ex. 32. *Libera domine populum* (folio 99).

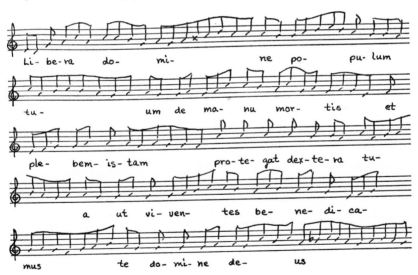

Li- be- ra do- mi- ne po- pu- lum

tu- um de ma- nu mor- tis et

ple- bem- is- tam pro-te- gat dex-te- ra tu-

a ut vi- ven- tes be- ne- di- ca-

mus te do- mi- ne de- us

Ex. 32 (continued).

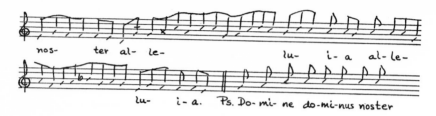

IV. *The Reception Processions*

To accompany an ecclesiastical dignitary into the church the respond, *Summae Trinitatis*, was sung; and to accompany a king, *Honor virtus*—the ninth and sixth responds of Matins on Trinity Sunday; for a queen, *Regnum mundi*, the last Matins respond of the Common of a virgin.

THE SPECIAL CEREMONIES

The following three antiphons accompanied the distribution of the blessed ashes on Ash Wednesday.

Ex. 33. *Exaudi nos domine quoniam* (folio 28v).

Ex. 34. *Iuxta vestibulum* (folio 29).

Iux- ta ves- ti- bu- lum et al-
ta- re plo- ra- bant sa- cer- do- tes
et le- vi- te mi- nis- tri do- mi-
ni et di- cent par- ce
do- mi- ne par- ce po- pu- lo tu-
o et ne dis- si- pes or- a
cla- manti- um ad te do- mi- ne.

Ex. 35. *Immutemur habitu* (folio 29).

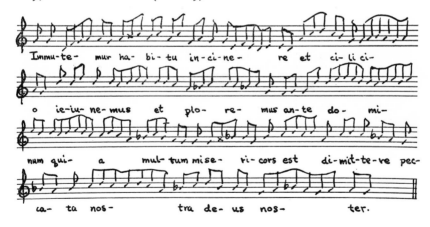

Immu- te- mur ha- bi- tu in- ci- ne- re et ci- li ci-
o ie- iu- ne- mus et plo- re- mus an- te do- mi-
num qui- a mul- tum mise- ri- cors est di- mit- te- re pec-
ca- ta nos- tra de- us nos- ter.

For the washing of the altars on Holy Thursday, the responds of the day's Matins were sung, with the Holy Week Vespers respond (*Circumdederunt me*) for the last altar. The versicle and prayer were those of the saint whose altar it was.

A hymn accompanied the clerk's adoration of the Cross on Good Friday; the special antiphon *Dum fabricator* (Folio 67v) was sung while the cross was being carried to the adoration of the people.

Ex. 36.

Ex. 36 (continued).

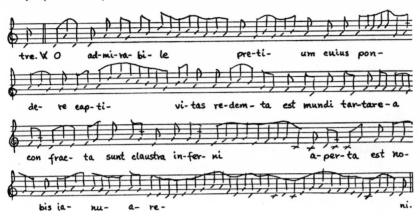

tre. ℣ O ad-mi-ra- bi- le pre-ti- um cuius pon-

de- re cap-ti- vi-tas re-dem- ta est mundi tar-tare-a

con frac- ta sunt claustra in-fer- ni a-per-ta est no-

bis ia- nu- a- re- ni.

IV. DEVELOPMENTS IN THE CUSTOMS AT SARUM

THE EARLY PRACTICE

Even in the relatively short period represented by the Sarum service books there were some changes and developments in the customs. None of the surviving Processionals—as we shall see later—can be earlier than the middle of the fourteenth century; but with the help of some older Sarum books which are concerned to some extent with the processions something can be said of the earlier practice.

The oldest source for the liturgical customs of Salisbury is a treatise which as come to be known as the Consuetudinary.[1] The oldest version,[2] a book which actually served in the Cathedral, must be from after 1173, for it provides for the Feast of the Martyrdom of St. Thomas of Canterbury.[3] But it does not include the Feast of St. Machutus, proclaimed in 1203,[4] nor the Feast of the Translation of St. Thomas, proclaimed in 1220,[5] which was probably taken up quickly at Sarum where the cult of this saint was very prominent.[6]

There survive, from about the same time, a Gradual and an Antiphoner, of the Sarum Use, but not from the Cathedral.

The Gradual[7] contains the Feast of St. Machutus, but does not yet have the Translation of St. Thomas. The rubrics make clear that it represents the Sarum practice:

[1] Edited by W. H. Frere in volume 1 of the *Use of* Sarum (Cambridge, 1898).

[2] This is kept in the Salisbury Diocesan Registry Office.

[3] Wilkins, *op. cit.*, I, 475. Frere discusses the development of the Sarum calendar in his introduction to the *Graduale Sarisburiense* (London, 1894), but in several instances his exposition is in disagreement with his references.

[4] By Innocent III. See Stadler and Heim, *Heiligenlexicon* (Augsburg, 1858-1882).

[5] Wilkins, *op. cit.*, I, 572.

[6] There had been an altar to the Saint even at Old Sarum. See the Treasurer's Inventory published by Wordsworth on page 179 ff. in his *Salisbury Processions and Ceremonies*. Richard Poore, Bishop of Salisbury, took part in the preparations for the translation of the Saint's body. The Translation is one of the feasts inserted "ex novo" in a later recension of the Consuetudinary (*ibid.*, 298; *The Use of Sarum*, I, 30).

[7] British Museum Ms add. 12194, published in facsimile by Frere (London, 1894) as *Graduale Sarisburiense*.

si vero in die cene ... evenerit, secundum consuetudinem ecclesie Sarum differatur ...[1]

The Antiphoner[2] is a little later, for it contains the Feast of the Translation of St. Thomas. But the Feast of St. Anianus, which was displaced in the calendar by that of St. Hugh after his canonization in 1220,[3] the Feast of the Relics, which was moved at Sarum to make way for the Octave of the Nativity—presumably about 1245[4]—and the Feast of Saints Primus and Felician, which was dislodged after 1248 by the Translation of St. Edmund of Canterbury,[5] are all found in their earlier places. The book seems to have been written for an Augustinian house: in it is found an office not in use at Sarum, "in natalis beatissimi patris nostri Augustini episcopi";[6] but it was the custom of the Austin Friars to follow the secular rite of the diocese.

The Consuetudinary lists the feasts "que habent processionem":

Die natalis domini
Die epiphanie
Purificatio beate Marie virginis
Die pasche
Dominica in albis
Die ascensionis domini
Die penthecostes
Festo sancte trinitatis
Assumpcione et Nativitate beate virginis Marie
Festo reliquiarum et omnium sanctorum
Dedicacio ecclesie et festo cuiuslibet ecclesie vel capelle;
Et in festo sancti Stephani
et sancti Johannis
et sanctorum Innocencium
et sancte Thome martyris in natali tempore;
Die circumcisionis
Nativitate sancti Johannis baptiste
Passione apostolorum petri et pauli

---

[1] Page 184 of the facsimile.

[2] Ms Mm 2 g of the University Library, Cambridge, published in facsimile by Frere (London, 1901-1925) as *Antiphonale Sarisburiense*.

[3] By Honorius III. See Stadler and Heim, *op cit.*, etc. Frere gives the year 1252 (*The Use of Sarum*, I, xx).

[4] The Octave was proclaimed by Innocent IV in a council at Lyons of that year. See E. I. Watkins, *The Church in Council* (London, 1960), 125. Frere gives the date of the proclamation as 1252.

[5] St. Edmund was canonized by Innocent IV in 1247 (Frere gives 1246) and his translation took place the following year. See Stadler and Heim, *op. cit.*, etc. This feast is also inserted "ex novo" in the later recension of the Consuetudinary.

[6] Page 501 of the facsimile.

Translacione sancti thome martyris
Festo sancti michaelis
Invencione sancte crucis.[1]

The last ten were to receive processions only when they fell upon Sunday.

Except for the three days following Easter and Pentecost, which of course could never include a Sunday,[2] and the Feasts of St. Andrew and Annunciation, this includes all the festivals listed subsequently[3] as doubles ("festa que sunt duplicia"). The late books give St. Andrew's Day as a minor double, but earlier, in the Customary (see below) it was assigned a lower rank. Perhaps at the time represented by the list of processions in the Consuetudinary it was a simple feast. Its later elevation is perfectly understandable, considering there was an altar to St. Andrew at Sarum. Annunciation was doubtless omitted unintentionally. There is no indication that this feast received the preferential treatment afforded it in the later books.

Neither the Consuetudinary nor the *Antiphonale* contains any indication that there were processions at First Vespers of the feasts of saints with altars in the church. Nor does the Consuetudinary give directions for a procession at First Vespers of the Feast of the Exaltation of the Cross.[4]

The older books specify a number of differences in the customs:

1. From the Consuetudinary account it appears that the banners on Palm Sunday were carried from the beginning with the main procession.[5] The *Graduale*—which must in this respect represent a still earlier practice —makes no mention whatever of a subsidiary procession.[6]

2. The Consuetudinary directs that on Holy Thursday the invitation to the penitents to return to the church is to be intoned by the arch-deacon. This is certainly a corruption of the text.[7] The arch-deacon would have just spoken to the bishop on behalf of the penitents; it makes no sense to have him reply to his own plea. The *Graduale* agrees with the Processional.

---

[1] Page 5 of the Frere edition. In the earliest version, the Treasurer is instructed to provide for double feasts with processions: "Simile servetur in omnibus festis duplicibus que habent processionem." (*loc. cit.*) The later manuscripts add "videlicet," and go on to list them.

[2] Henderson, in the introduction to his edition of the Processional, unaccountably lists these days with those having processions.

[3] *Ibid.*, 29.

[4] This procession is found in the *Antiphonale*.

[5] Frere, *The Use of Sarum*, I, 59.

[6] The provisions for Palm Sunday are found on page 79 and following in the facsimile.

[7] Frere, *The Use of Sarum*, I, 144. The whole passage is doubtful.

3. On Holy Saturday, at the consecration of the font, there was no thurifer; and only one boy, who carried the candle used in the blessing *after* the bearers of the oil and chrism.[1]

4. At the procession on Easter morning before Matins only one thurifer is prescribed.[2] The *Antiphonale* agrees with the Processional and requires two.

5. The procession before Mass on Easter Sunday, according to the Consuetudinary, remained within the church and cloister as on Christmas and most of the double feasts.[3]

6. On St. Mark's Day for the Major Litany, on the Rogation Days, and when there was a procession of reception the church was left and re-entered by the south door[4] (on other days when the procession left the church it was by the west door, as in all such cases in the Processional).

A few practices of the Processional are not found in the early books: (1) the carrying of an extra Gospel text in processions for double feasts, (2) the carrying of the candle reserved for the Holy Saturday consecration of the font in the procession for the Feast of the Purification, and (3) the kissing of the bishop's hand by the penitents as they leave the church on Ash Wednesday.

The old books choose different pieces to be sung in the processions in a number of cases.

The "Ecce advenit" prescribed by the Consuetudinary for the procession on Ash Wednesday[5] is doubtless a mis-reading for *Ecce Adam*, the usual respond. However, a significant variation is this book's choice of *Christus resurgens*[6] for the Vespers procession of the Feast of the Discovery of the Cross. The *Antiphonale* for both these occasions agrees with the Processional.

The *Graduale*, for the Sixth Day of Christmas, provides a choice of pieces.[7] First are given those of the Processional, the expected pieces for a procession within the Octave of Christmas; but in addition, the processional respond and antiphon for the return to the choir of the Circum-

---

[1] *Ibid.*, 150.

[2] *Ibid.*, 153.

[3] *Ibid.*, 156. Compare the directions for the procession on Ascension Thursday, *ibid.*, 175.

[4] *Ibid.*, 172, 173, 205. The later change was doubtless owing to the addition of the cloister c. 1263-1284.

[5] *Ibid.*, 138.

[6] *Ibid.*, 164.

[7] Page 18 in the facsimile.

cision procession in anticipation of that feast. The versicle and prayer, no matter which chants were used, were those of Christmas. For Sexagesima,[1] *Volens Noe scire*, the eighth Matins respond and respond of first Vespers, and for Quinquagesima,[2] *Revertenti Abraham*, the second Matins respond and respond of first Vespers, are given in place of the later choice, the ninth Matins respond. The respond *Emendemus in melius* is not among those provided for the lenten ferial processions.

The *Antiphonale* provides a Marian Antiphon (*O gloriosa genetrix*)[3] which is not included in the Processional.

For the Commemorations of the Virgin sung at the return to the choir the choice was not settled. For the processions at Matins and Vespers in Paschal time the older books allow a choice of any of the Marian Antiphons where the Processional is specific. At Matins and Vespers on Easter and in Easter Week the Consuetudinary[4] specifies *Post partum*, the Matins memorial versicle. The *Antiphonale* and *Graduale* allow a choice between *Post partum* and *Sancta dei genetrix*, the Vespers memorial versicle, at both the Matins and Mass Processions in the summer period.

The *Graduale* and *Antiphonale* allow a similar freedom in the choice of prayer: for the processions at Vespers and before Mass in the period from Trinity Sunday to Advent, any of *Concede quaesumus* (as in the Processional), *Famulorum tuorum quaesumus domine*, and *Omnipotens sempiterne deus nos famulos tuos*—that is, a choice of any of the usual prayers for the current memorial of the Virgin at Vespers and Matins.

Ms Harl. 1001 of the British Museum is an "Ordinale Sarum" with an appended set of "Addiciones."[5] The addenda begin with 1278, for they have the following preface:

> Quia multi defectus reperiuntur in ordinale Sarum usus, quem nos habemus, super multis articulis subscriptis, Succentor dicte ecclesie Sarum, mediante quodam speciali, rogatus per strictam examinacionem certificavit VIII° Iduum Marcii Anno Domini M° CC° LXX° octavo.

But this date does not hold for all; one of the later directions[6] quotes from a decree of Boniface VIII raising the feasts of the four Latin Doctors

---

[1] *Ibid.*, 26.

[2] *Ibid.*, 27.

[3] Pages 295, 530 of the facsimile.

[4] Frere, *The Use of Sarum*, I, 158, 160.

[5] Edited by Frere in volume II of *The Use of Sarum*.

[6] *Ibid.*, 206.

to double rank, part of the *Liber Sextus Decretalium* of 1298[1] and can scarcely be from before the fourteenth century.

The main body of the ordinal contains the Translation of St. Richard, who was canonized in 1262,[2] and some of the corrections of the *addiciones*, but not yet Corpus Christi, proclaimed in 1264,[3] or the direction from the Sext; and from this it appears that it represents the usage of the late thirteenth century.[4]

This book, usually called the Old Ordinal,[5] shows some of the changes brought about since the early part of the century, changes which bring the customs closer to those of the Processional.

First there is the matter of the occasions for processions. The Old Ordinal adds to those of the Consuetudinary, processions at Mass and at Vespers for St. Kathrine, St. Andrew, and for all saints with altars in the church. By the time of the *addiciones*, the feasts had been assigned subtler ranks, principal double, major double, minor double, and so on.[6] The feasts which were entitled to processions whatever day they occurred with one exception are classed as principal or major doubles; those which had processions only on Sundays are listed as minor doubles. The Annunciation was a minor double, but as one of the feasts "in cuius honor fundata est ecclesia"[7] (in whose honour the church was founded) it was treated at Sarum like those of higher rank.

Some of the differences between the early and late books are resolved. The Old Ordinal agrees with the Processional about the constitution of the processions on Holy Thursday and Easter Morning. But for Palm Sunday, the same directions are given as in the *Graduale*. On the other questions of ceremony the ordinal and the *addiciones* are silent.

---

[1] *Ibid.*, xvii, note 1; and "Sext" in the *Oxford Dictionary of the Christian Church* (edited by F. L. Cross, Oxford, 1957).

[2] By Urban IV. See the *Dictionary of the Christian Church*, 1164.

[3] Also by Urban IV, *ibid.*, 345. This feast was accepted slowly elsewhere and may have been late coming to Sarum. It is not mentioned in the *addiciones* to the Old Gradual.

[4] That is, in its present form. But the rubrics of the *Graduale* seem to have been taken from some form of this Ordinal. Cf. the *Graduale*, p. 79 ff., and Frere, *The Use of Sarum*, II, 161.

[5] A marginal note explains a passage crossed out: "non habetur in novo ordinale" (not included in the new ordinal).

[6] *Ibid.*, 205-206.

[7] Conception is not mentioned in the early books. This feast was kept from the eleventh century in English Benedictine houses, (Baudot, *The Roman Breviary*, [London, 1909] 253 ff.) but apparently not until much later at Sarum. The Customary (see below) seems to be the earliest book to provide for it (Frere, *op. cit.*, 30) and there it is treated out of place as though it were recently added.

The Old Ordinal allows the same freedom in the choice of antiphons, versicles, and prayers for the commemorations of the Virgin at processions as the earlier books; and agrees with the Consuetudinary in specifying the versicle *Post partum* for the Matins and Vespers processions of Easter and Easter Week. For Sexagesima and Quinquagesima the same responds are given as in the *Graduale*, but those of the Processional are offered as alternatives.[1] In the remaining cases where the older books differed, viz for the Octave of Christmas, Ash Wednesday, the Feast of the Discovery of the Cross, and the ferial processions of Lent, the Old Ordinal agrees with the Processional.

For some of the new processions, however, the prayers were not settled. At first Vespers of St. Lawrence a choice of three is allowed: *Da quaesumus* (as in the Processional), *Letitur ecclesia*, or *Beati Laurencii*.[2] For first Vespers of St. Michael the Old Ordinal first had *Perpetuum nobis domine*,[3] but this was later changed in the margin to *Beatus Michaelis archangeli*[4] (probably more correctly, *Beati Michaelis*, the Processional prayer[5]).

The Customary[6] is best described as an adaptation of the Consuetudinary for parish churches, and covers almost the same ground as that book. But as it survives it must be later than any of the texts which have been considered, for it incorporates the Sext decrees of 1298.

Two further feasts were added to the roll in this book: Corpus Christi, with the rank of major double, and Conception as a minor double. There is no indication in the Customary that Conception and Annunciation were given processions except on Sunday. This is the earliest book to prescribe a wooden cross without a crucifix in the Sunday processions of Lent[7] and two texts of the Gospel carried on cushions for double feasts.[8]

A second Sarum ordinal,[9] usually referred to as the "New Ordinal"

---

[1] As in the Processional of the National Library of Scotland, Ms 18.5.20.

[2] Frere, *The Use of Sarum*, II, 123. Only cues are given for these prayers, but the second seems to be *Letitur ecclesia tua deus beati N.* from the Common of a martyr (*The Sarum Missal*, edited by J. W. Legg [Oxford, 1916], 359, note 3), and the third, *Beati Laurencii martyris tui*, the Secret of the Mass of the Octave of St. Lawrence (ibid., 310).

[3] Probably a cue for the Collect of the *Missa de Angelis* (ibid., 459).

[4] Frere, *The Use of Sarum*, II, 131.

[5] There is some disagreement in the Processionals about the order of the opening words of this prayer. In some it begins: "Beati archangeli tui Michaelis."

[6] Edited by Frere in *The Use of Sarum*, vol I.

[7] *Ibid.*, 219.

[8] *Ibid.*, 64.

[9] The first few pages of the New Ordinal are printed by Frere (*ibid.*, II, 208 ff.) from British Museum Ms Harl. 2911, and Ms 44 of Corpus Christi College, Oxford.

because of a reference it contains to an "antiquum ordinale" it super-seded,[1] survives in several manuscript copies.[2] This book is of special interest, not for the customs it describes—which are the same as in the earliest processionals—but because it is, unmistakably, a direct source of the Processional, and provides an approximate *terminus post quem* for its compilation.

The Relationship of the Processional and the New Ordinal

All the later service books of Sarum owe their rubrics to the New Ordinal. The *verbatim* agreement in the directions for the ceremonies makes this unequivocal. In the case of the Processional the debt is much greater and accounts for certain peculiarities in format. A comparison with the Calendar will show that the *sanctorale* of the Processional does not contain all the services required in the course of the year. Lacking are processions for more than twenty saints whose feasts, no matter what Easter's date, fell well within the allowed periods. The Offices of all but two of these feasts were taken from the Common; and their processions were intended to be performed from the *Commune Sanctorum* provided in the Processional. The curious features are these:

1. the *sanctorale* does provide, individually and unnecessarily, for nearly as many saints whose services were taken from the Common;

2. it omits processions for St. Andrew and for the Feast of the Discovery of St. Stephen, and

3. assigns a respond from the Common for St. Agatha—even though there were proper responds for these three occasions. The New Ordinal provides for, or omits, exactly the same saints; and contains the same irregularities found in the Processional.

The Date of the New Ordinal

It seems likely that the "antiquum ordinale" supplanted by this book was the one from Ms Harl. 1001 just considered; in any case, the present one is later, for it provides for Corpus Christi. The New Ordinal is clearly

[1] Ms Harl. 2911, folio 107; Frere, *The Use of Sarum* II, 229. The passage is quoted below. Frere seems to have believed that this reference was found also in the Corpus Christi manu-script, but it is not. There are a number of other cases where Frere's printed text misrepresents this source.

[2] Corpus Christi College, Oxford, Ms 44; Ms 175 of Sarum Cathedral; British Museum Ms Harl. 2911; British Museum Ms Arundel 130.

subsequent to an "ordinale Welbyk" mentioned in the Ms Harl. 2911 copy;[1] and this treatise, if the author was the Thomas de Welewick who was precentor at Sarum from 1341 to 1343,[2] can scarcely have been obsolete before the middle of the century. However, the New Ordinal cannot have been long after, for it makes no provisions for the Feast of St. Anne; and since the papal proclamation prompted by the marriage of an English monarch would not have been ignored in the major revision of the customs that the book represents, it must have been drawn up before 1383.

Other evidence points to the same period. A passage in a tract by Wycliffe, believed to have been written between 1365 and 1375, refers to a major revision of the Sarum Use,[3] and, as likely as not, alludes to the Processional itself:

> Ah Lord, yif alle the studie and traveile that men han now about Salisbury uss with multitude of newe costy portos, antifeners, graielis and alle othere bokis weren turned in-to makynge of biblis...

The changes in the processions at Sarum—in keeping with the changes in the liturgical customs in general—tended toward proliferation of services, greater complexity, and the closer integration of components. In the time between the earliest service books and the formulation of the New Use, processions became more frequent, symbolically more meaningful, and more closely affiliated with the Daily Office.

At the end of the twelfth century festive processions before the High Mass were held only on Sundays and on ten of the greatest feasts. This is fewer by several than in the late Processionals. But compared with the later practice the difference in the number of processions is not so striking as the difference in the number of nominal occasions for them. It was only feasts of double rank whose services were entitled to displace the Sunday service and procession. Consequently the number of festivals which might have processions made up in their honour was less than a third of what it was to be. A processional in the early years would have been a very much smaller book.

---

[1] "Sed nuper post terciam ... secundum antiquum ordinale et ordinale Welbyk..." (folio 107, Ms Harl. 2911). According to Frere (*The Use of Sarum*, II, 229; cf. Introduction, xi) the Corpus Christi manuscript refers to an "ordinale Wellwyk". In fact, there is only the "Welbyk" reference, and that only in Ms Harl. 2911.

[2] Frere, *The Use of Sarum*, II, xx.

[3] "Of Feyned Contemplatif Lif...," discussed by Chr. Wordsworth in his *The Tracts of Clement Maydeston* (for the Henry Bradshaw Society, London, 1894), xvi. Wycliffe died in 1384.

In the four centuries that followed, the number of occasions for processions increased more sharply than would be expected from the natural growth of the Calendar. New feasts were nearly always assigned higher ranks than they would have received formerly; and by way of compensation, older feasts tended either to be promoted in rank—as they were for the four Latin Doctors—or awarded certain of the distinctions—including processions—of the great festivals. By the latter part of the thirteenth century the list of double feasts had become much longer. In the following century the privilege of displacing the dominical service was extended to all feasts with nine lections at Matins, and finally, to any three-lection feast for which the choir was ruled.

The Vespers processions for the feasts of saints with altars in the church, and the Vespers procession to the Rood for the Feast of the Exaltation of the Cross appear to have been innovations of the thirteenth century. The latter was plainly an extension of the similar procession for the Feast of the Discovery of the Cross; although the Paschal prayer was appropriate only for the first occasion, which fell in Eastertide, the same pieces were sung for both. This irregularity was later to be straightened out. Similarly, the procession at Vespers on the Feast of the Discovery of the Cross appears to have been an extension of those on Saturdays in Paschal Time. The earlier version of the procession for the Feast used the same pieces as the others.

This line of reasoning can be carried further by extrapolation. It seems likely that the processions to the rood on Saturdays during the summer were prompted by their analogues in Paschal Time; and they, in turn, by the ancient Vespers processions of Easter and its Octave. The Vespers processions for the altar saints—in the case of Sarum—were likely imported from another church, but their origin is probably found in the earlier and similar processions of Christmas Week. These would have been suggested by the occurrence at the close of Vespers of memorials of the saints concerned.

A number of the late developments in the processions were refinements of form in the interest of a more effective symbolism. Double feasts had previously been indicated by three crosses in the processions before Mass; simple feasts by a single cross. But with the subtler ranks assigned feasts in the fourteenth century came subtler distinctions: the later books require three crosses on principal and major doubles, two for minor doubles; in Lent the cross was to be plain, of wood, and without a crucifix. On simple feasts a single text of the Gospel was to be carried "ex directo pectore" (right against the breast) by the sub-deacon; on double feasts both the deacon and sub-deacon were to carry Gospels, upon cushions.

The procession that underwent the most change at Sarum is the most elaborate of all: Palm Sunday's. In the earliest version, used in the twelfth century and probably from the founding of the Diocese, the triumphal entry of Jesus into Jerusalem was simply related in the texts of the antiphons and in the Gospel account read at the first station in the church yard. In a later version, perhaps still from the twelfth century, the biblical events are dramatized. Christ, represented in the consecrated Host, is carried in a separate procession to approach the assembled people and clergy at the close of the Gospel reading, just at the words, "Blessed is he who comes in the name of the Lord." There is no trace of the next development until the middle of the fourteenth century. By then the banners and the festive crucifix were reserved and introduced in the second procession with the Host. The result was the dramatic transformation *en route* of a lenten penitential procession into a procession of triumph. The final form of the Palm Sunday procession is not met until the sixteenth century in the printed Processionals.

In the thirteenth and fourteenth centuries, chants and prayers were substituted in a number of the processions. Most of these changes, as will have been noticed, served to bring the choice into line with the system governing the other processions, or to establish a closer rapport with the Daily Office.

For Quinquagesima and Sexagesima Sundays there was an intermediate period during which the old choice for the processions remained an alternative. This is doubtless also the explanation for the two responds offered in the earliest Sarum book for the procession of the Octave of Christmas.

It was not until the revision which produced the New Use in the fourteenth century that the commemorations of the Virgin sung in the processions were brought into correspondence with the Office memorials. Previously there had been no attempt to restrict the Matins versicle to morning processions and the Vespers versicle to processions in the evening. There is no question that *Post partum* and *Sancta dei genetrix* had specific assignments in the Office in the early years. The Old Ordinal says, plainly:

> versiculus ad vesperas, *Sancta dei genetrix*
> versiculus ad matutinas, *Post partum virgo*.[1]

---

[1] *Ed. cit.*, 93.

And the same provisions were made in Bodley Ms Rawl. C 73, a Sarum Breviary of the early thirteenth century.

THE LATER PRACTICE

From the first appearance of the Processional to the disappearance of the Sarum Rite after the death of Mary in 1558 the processional customs changed very little. The Processional was never officially revised. It had inherited from the New Ordinal the defects already noted: deficiencies for St. Andrew, St. Agatha, and for the Feast of the Discovery of St. Stephen; and, directly or indirectly, the inconsistency between its general rubrics and the contents of the *sanctorale* over the feasts which were to have processions. Individual manuscript processionals were occasionally corrected. Ms Harl. 2945 has the general rubric brought up to date, and calls for processions:

> in omnibus festis sanctorum cum regimine chori qui in dominicis contigerunt...[1] (for all saints' feasts which fall on Sunday and which have the choir ruled).

Several others add the services for St. Andrew and St. Stephen. But none of the corrections were incorporated in the printed Processionals of the sixteenth century. In fact, later additions to the customs brought more anomalies.

The introduction of the feast of St. Anne in 1383 caused no difficulty. It was given a procession in keeping with the rubrics for a simple feast with nine lections. But the processions for two of the *nova festa* were composed in disregard for the rubrics. They specify that the pieces sung in processions on feasts with the rank of major double or higher will be "totum de sancto" (all from the saint's office). The Feast of the Visitation and the Feast of the Holy Name were assigned the rank of major doubles,[2] but the pieces prescribed for the return of the procession to the choir were, for the first feast, in commemoration of All Saints, and for the second, in commemoration of the Virgin.

There were a few late changes and additions to the customs.

1. The latest manuscripts and all the editions substitute the Collect of the Votive Mass of the Holy Cross for the Paschal memorial prayer in the Vespers procession for the Feast of the Exaltation of the Cross. This latter prayer was inappropriate in September.

[1] Folio 109 v.
[2] See the calendar of the 1531 edition of the Breviary in Proctor and Wordsworth, *op. cit.*, I, x.

2. For Holy Thursday's Maundy Service, the editions of 1502, 1508, and 1517 provide a Common to accommodate the altars in any church. Prayers are given for their washing in descending order of importance: first the High Altar, then the altar of the Holy Trinity, St. Michael, the Holy Apostles, the Holy Martyrs, the Holy Confessors, the Holy Virgins, and the superaltar[1] in the vestibule.

3. For the Feast of the Annunciation, for the return of the procession to the choir, all the editions provide—in addition to the pieces *de omnibus sanctis* and *in tempore paschali*, which are found in the earlier processionals —an antiphon, versicle and prayer *de sancto*, doubtless for churches dedicated to the Virgin. Feasts of the patron, it will be remembered, had locally the rank of principal double.

4. The final development in the Sarum Palm Sunday procession brought it close to the liturgical drama. In all the editions, excepting that of 1502, an introductory verse, "Hierusalem respice ad orientem" was added to the hymn *En rex venit*. This verse was to be sung by a boy dressed, or rather costumed, as a prophet.[2]

It may seem odd that the late Processionals, or at least the printed editions, which presumably represented the official Sarum Rite, do not contain services for more of the late Sarum feasts. It would not be so surprising that the advent of the feasts of St. David, St. Chad, and St. Winifred in 1545,[3] or St. Frideswide in 1480[4] made no impression on the Processional. Most of the office for these saints was from the Common, and their procession could have been performed from the Processional's *Commune Sanctorum* as were those of so many other saints. But the Processional never included a service for the feast of the Translation of St. Osmund, even though it was held at Sarum from 1457[5] and did have proper responds. The fact is, that by the middle of the fifteenth century the Sarum Use was no longer dictated from the Cathedral. Only feasts universally celebrated were now added to the official Use. There can be no doubt that the feast and the procession of the Translation of St. Osmund were held at Salisbury.[6] Yet the calendar of the printed Sarum

---

[1] Apparently a portable altar stored in the vestibule.
[2] For the costuming and possible origins of the prophet's part in the Palm Sunday procession see Young, *The Drama of the Medieval Church*, (Oxford, 1933) I, 93, 549-550.
[3] Wilkins, *op. cit.*, III, 375.
[4] *Ibid.*, III, 613.
[5] *Lincoln Cathedral Statutes*, vol. III part 2, 846.
[6] Ms 148 of the Cathedral, folio 36 v.

Breviary of 1531[1] gives this festival as "non Sarum." The Sarum Use had become a national use; and the practice of Salisbury Cathedral itself could be treated as a local variation.

The Reformation did not leave the processional customs or the Processional unchanged. In 1541 a new, emended Breviary was issued "in quo nomen Romano pontifici falso adscriptum omittitur, una cum aliis que Christianissimo nostri Regis statuto repugnant"[2] (in which the falsely included name of the Roman Pope is omitted, along with all others [e.g. St. Thomas of Canterbury] repugnant to the injunction of our most Christian King). This kind of emendation reached the Processional as well. Where the early editions had read "Oremus pro ecclesia Romana et pro papa et archiepiscopus..." (Let us pray for the Roman Church, for the Pope, and for the Archbishop), that of 1544 read "Oremus pro ecclesia Anglicana et pro rege nostro et archiepiscopus..." (Let us pray for the English Church, for our King, and the Archbishop). The service for St. Thomas of Canterbury was omitted in this edition, and either omitted or erased in those up to 1555.

There were attempts to reform the Processional further. In 1544 Cranmer wrote to Henry VIII: "According to your highness commandment... I have translated into the English tongue ... certain processions to be used on festival days ..."[3] Cranmer was engaged on more than a translation, for in the same letter he says: "I was constrained to use more than the liberty of a translator: for in some processions I have altered divers words; in some I have added part; in some taken away ...," and later: "The song that shall be made thereunto (i.e. to his translations) would not be full of notes, but as near as may be, for every syllable a note..."

In spite of Cranmer's attempts, the English Processional was never approved. The next year, in 1545, Henry seems to have issued an Injunction which made the litany, in English, the sole accompaniment to processions, and thereby abolished the Processional. A chronicler reported:

> The eighteenth of october, being Sainct Lukes daie and Soundaie, [St.] Paules quire song the procession in English by the Kings iniunction, which shall be song in everie parish church throughout Englande everie Soundaie and festival daie, and non other.[4]

[1] *Breviarium ... Sarum, ed. cit.*, I, (ix).

[2] F. E. Brightman, *The English Rite* (2 vols., London, 1915), I, lvii-lviii.

[3] *Ibid.*, lxii.

[4] From Wriothesley's Chronicle, quoted by Brightman, *op. cit.*, lxii.

Two years later, Edward VI abolished all processions except those in Rogationtide in the twenty-fourth of the Royal Injunctions of August 1547:

> They shall not from henceforth ... at any time, use any procession about the church or churchyard, or any other place, but immediately before high mass the priest with other of the choir shall kneel in the midst of the church, and sing or say plainly and distinctly the litany ... and none other procession or litany is to be had or used but the said litany in English.[1]

Queen Mary's first act of repeal in 1553 maintained the substitution of the English Litany for the Processional; but it was restored by the eleventh of the Injunctions of March 1553-1554.[2] As a result, the *Processionale* was published again in 1554, although still with the emended text. The original text was restored in the edition of 1555, and continued to be issued until 1558. But after the death of Mary in that year, the liturgical practice of Edward VI was brought back, and the Processional fell into disuse.

---

[1] *Ibid.*, lxii. See also "Injunction" in *The Oxford Dictionary of the Christian Church.*
[2] *The English Rite*, I, clxv. In England, at this time, the new year was reckoned from the twenty-fifth of March. See H. Nicolas, *The Chronology of History* (London, 1838), 41.

PART TWO

THE GENERAL PRACTICE

V. THE SOURCES FOR
THE GENERAL PRACTICE

It has long been supposed that the processional was a very recent book. DuCange, in his *Glossarium* (1678) wrote that he knew of none earlier than the seventeenth century; and the Benedictines under the direction of Dom Carpentier, preparing a second edition in 1734, knew nothing to disturb this date. As recent a writer as Henri Leclercq, in the *Dictionnaire d'archéologie et de liturgie*,[1] wrote that processionals did not appear before the very end of the Middle Ages.

Actually, they are much older than has been supposed. From early library catalogues[2] it can be shown that the processional was common in the larger and more important churches from the thirteenth century. The fact remains, however, that it was one of the latest of the service books to come into use. A number of early references such as, "anti-phonam cantando in processione sicut continet Antiphonarius"[3] (singing the antiphon in procession as it is found in the Antiphoner) from the eighth century, and, "tunc vadant... canentes antiphonas quae in Anti-phonario continentur"[4] (then they are to walk forth singing the antiphons which are contained in the Antiphoner) from the tenth, attest to the absence of any special book for the processions. Examples before the thirteenth century are rare, and evidence for them can be found for scarcely a century before.

Long before they can be found in separate collections the processional chants were included in the books of the Mass and Office. Whether these books were carried in the processions is not clear. The tropers are easily portable; and the others, although not handbooks, are usually not so large that it would have been impractical to walk with them. But even if we assume that the books were carried, one alone could not have relieved

---

[1] Ed. F. Cabrol (Paris, 1903-1953).
[2] P. Gy, "Collectaire, rituel, processionel," in *Revue des sciences philosophiques et théologiques*, XLIV, (1960) 466.
[3] *Ordo* XX of the *Ordines Romani* (ed. by M. Andrieu in 5 vols in the series *Specilegium Sacrum Louvaniense*, 1931-1961), III, 113.
[4] Number 9 of the sources, 32-33.

the whole choir of the burden of memorization—nor, for that matter, could two or three. And it is quite certain that multiple copies in precious parchment are out of the question for the early Middle Ages. Quite possibly, on some occasions, the choir rulers did sing in the processions from one or two copies; but we must suppose that for the most part during this period the processional chants were sung from memory. Even in 1472, when the requirements might be expected to have been less stringent, the vicars at Salisbury were supposed to know, as part of the conditions of admission to office, all the antiphons of the *temporale* and *sanctorale*.[1] At Lincoln in 1236 every vicar had to know by heart the entire Antiphonal and Hymnal[2].

The sources vary widely in the amount of information they yield. The service books of the Mass and Office give, at most, bare, often unsatisfactory indications for the processions. The ordinals, which did not appear much before the twelfth century, are very often not at all complete for the processions. The earlier ones especially will often omit basic information about their form or route, or will refer summarily in a rubric such as "postea fiat processio ut in processionalibus habetur"[3] to books long since vanished. The Sarum Processional was complete in itself for all of the liturgy celebrated away from the choir, and contained not only the chants and prayers, but relevant directions extracted from the Ordinal. But this was most unusual. Many of the processionals are simple chant books, and sometimes very scanty.

Some sources omit processions which were in fact customary. It is to be expected that Graduals might not be concerned with ceremonies of the Office, and that Antiphoners might ignore those of the Mass. But it seems that the processionals themselves cannot always be relied upon to represent the whole practice of the churches which owned them. The processional from St. Arnulph's, Metz, and the first one of the two from Bury St. Edmund's contain no provisions for processions at Vespers.[4] But nearly contemporary sources from each place, the Metz ordinal and the second Bury St. Edmund's processional,[5] do. It is extremely unlikely that in both cases these processions were innovations in the brief period separating the two sources for each church.

---

[1] See the rules laid down by Bishop Beauchamp, Wordsworth, *op. cit.*, 274-275.
[2] *Lincoln Cathedral Statutes*, ed. H. Bradshaw and Chr. Wordsworth (3 vols, 1892-1897), II, 145.
[3] The Exeter Ordinal (number 71), page 324.
[4] Sources 54, 70.
[5] Sources 55, 82.

Although, as would be expected, there are more processionals surviving from the fifteenth than from the previous centuries, there are surprisingly few from the sixteenth and after. The advent of printing made copies cheaper and more plentiful than manuscripts; but paper books were also less durable and less treasured. Besides, a decline of the Gregorian musical tradition coincided with a decline in elaborate ritual, so that the centuries closing the Middle Ages and beginning the Renaissance saw almost everywhere the disappearance of all but a few of the processions. By the eighteenth century a processional was not counted among a church's necessary service books.

The dating of the sources, where it is simply stated, is from official library catalogues, or from editors' notes. Dates for the Bodleian manuscripts are taken not from the published catalogue, but from one more recent, in manuscript, prepared for the Library by S. J. P. Van Dijk in 1951, and on deposit in the reading room.

Extracts concerned with the processions from ordinals and other similar books—many of them no longer extant—have been included by the liturgist Edmond Martène in his *De antiquis ecclesiae ritibus* (1700-1702).[1]

"Antiphoner" and "Gradual," except to conform to the titles of editions, have been used in the modern sense to refer to books of the Office and Mass respectively.

Seventh Century

1. León (northern Spain)

   Gradual; Archivos de la Catedral (no number); published in facsimile with a text edition as *Antiphonario Visigotico Mozarabe de la Catedral de León* (ed. L. Brou and J. Vives [Madrid, 1953-1959]). The manuscript was written in the first half of the tenth century, but apparently copied from a book dating from the end of the seventh (José Vives, "Datación del Antifonario Legionense" in *Hispania Sacra* [Instituto P. Enrique Flórez, Barcelona-Madrid], VIII [1955], 117-124; Louis Brou, "L'Antiphonaire grégorien au début du VIII° siècle" in *Anuario Musical*, V [Barcelona, 1950], 3ff.). It is certain that

---

[1] See especially III, 177 ff.; IV, 45 ff., 280 ff. in the Venice edition of 1738.

nothing was added to the book by the scribe, for he makes it clear in a prologue that the chants he was copying were no longer current:

Disparesque modos nunc te eclesia canet
finitam habentes hanc artem prefulgidam (*ed. cit.*, I, 5).

Eighth-ninth Century

2. Saint-Riquier (between Amiens and Boulogne)
   "Instituto Sancti Angilberti Abbatis [d. 814] de Diversitate Officiorum"; ed. Edmund Bishop in *Liturgica Historica* (Oxford, 1918), 321 ff.
3. Mont-Blandin (near Ghent)
   Gradual; Brussels, Bibl. Royale Ms 10127-10144. This and the following three text manuscripts of the Gradual have been edited by René Jean Hesbert in *Antiphonale Missarum Sextuplex* (Paris, 1935).

Ninth Century

4. Compiègne (near Soissons)
   Gradual; Paris, Bibliothèque Nationale, fonds Latin, Ms 17436.
5. Antiphoner; in the same manuscript as the preceeding; published in *Patrologia Latina*, LXVIII.
6. Senlis (north of Paris)
   Gradual; Paris, Bibl. Ste-Geneviève, Ms 111.

Ninth-Tenth Century

7. Corbie (near Amiens)
   Gradual; Paris, Bibl. Nat. lat. 12050.
8. Laon (north-east of Rheims)
   Gradual; Codex 239 of the Bibl. Municipale of Laon; published in facsimile by the Benedictines of Solesmes as vol. X (1909) of the series *Paléographie Musicale* (Tournai-Solesmes, 1889-   ).

Tenth Century

(ENGLAND)

9. English Benedictine Houses
   Customary; drawn up at Winchester and Canterbury; British

Museum Ms Tiberius A. 3; *circa* A. D. 970; edited by T. Symons as *Regularis Concordia* (London, 1952).

10. Chartres
    Gradual; Codex 47 of the Bibl. Munic. of Chartres; published in facsimile as vol. XI (1912) of *Paléographie Musicale*.
11. Limoges
    Troper; Abbey of St. Martial; Paris, Bibl. Nat. lat. Ms 1240; A. D. 933-936 (see G. Suñol, *Introduction à la paléographie musicale* [Paris, 1935], 268).
12. Rénaud
    Gradual-Antiphoner; manuscript from a private (anonymous) collection; published in facsimile as vol. XVI (1955-56) of *Paléographie Musicale*.

(GERMANIC REGIONS)

13. Mainz
    Troper; British Museum Ms add. 19768; A.D. 960.
14. St. Gall (north-central Switzerland)
    Antiphoner; St. Gall Stiftsbibliothek Ms 390-391; published in facsimile as vol. I, second series (1900) of *Paléographie Musicale*.
15. Gradual; St. Gall Stiftsbibliothek Ms 339; published in facsimile as vol. I (1889) of *Paléographie Musicale*.

Tenth-Eleventh Century

(FRANCE)

16. Limoges
    Troper; Abbey of St. Martial; Paris, Bibl. Nat. lat. 1120; from the appearance of the notation this manuscript seems to be a little earlier than the following.
17. Troper; Abbey of St. Martial; Paris, Bibl. Nat. lat. 1121; A.D. 994-1033.
18. Montpellier
    Gradual-Tonary; Codex H. 159 of the Faculty of Medicine, Montpellier; published in facsimile as vol. VIII (1901) of *Paléographie Musicale*.

19. Einsiedeln (central Switzerland)
    Gradual; Einsiedeln Stiftsbibliothek Ms 121; published in facsimile as volume IV (1894) of *Paléographie Musicale.*

Eleventh Century

20. Canterbury
    Customary; edited by M. Knowles as *Decreta Lanfranci* (London, 1951) after Ms B IV 24 of the Durham Cathedral Chapter Library.

(FRANCE)

21. Cluny
    Consuetudines Cluniacenses; Patrologia Latina, CXLIX, 643 ff.; A.D. 1086.
22. Rouen
    Liber de Officiis Ecclesiasticis ad Maurilium Rotomagensis Archiepiscopus of John of Avranches; edited in *Patrologia Latina,* CXLVII, 9 ff.
23. Saint-Yrieix (near Limoges)
    Gradual; Paris, Bibl. Nat. lat. Ms 903; published in facsimile as volume XIII (1925) of *Paléographie Musicale.* The edition does not include a large number of processional antiphons found at the end of the manuscript.
24. Toulouse
    Gradual; British Museum, Ms Harleian 4951.

(ITALY)

25. Benevento (north-east of Naples)
    Gradual; Rome, Bibl. Vaticana Ms lat. 10673; published in facsimile as vol. XIV (1931) of *Paléographie Musicale.*
26. Nonantola (near Modena)
    Troper; Bologna University Ms 2824; published in facsimile by Vecchi as *Troparium Sequentiarum Nonantularum* (Modena, 1955).
27. Novalesa (west of Turin)
    Troper; Oxford, Bodleian Ms Douce 222; second half of the century.

Eleventh-Twelfth Century

(ITALY)

28. Benevento

Gradual-Proser-Troper; Codex VI. 34 of the Chapter Library, Benevento; published in facsimile as vol. XV (1937) of *Paléographie Musicale*.

29. Pontetetto (near Lucca)
Processional; Ms 609 of the Chapter Library, Lucca.
30. Rome
Gradual; Bibl. Vaticana lat. Ms 5319.

Twelfth Century

(ENGLAND)

31. Gloucester-Hereford
Antiphoner-Kyriale-Processional; St. Peter's (Gloucester), St. Guthlac's (Hereford); Oxford, Jesus College Ms 10; late in the century.
32. Tynemouth (northern England)
Processional; Oxford, Bodleian Ms Laud Misc. 4; A.D. 1154-1179 (see E. Nicholson, *Early Bodleian Music* (London, 1901, III).

(FRANCE)

33. Auxerre (south of Paris)
Gradual; Paris, Bibl. Nat. lat. Ms 10511; end of the century.
34. Toulouse
Processional; St. Saturnin's; Madrid, Bibl. Nat. Ms C 131. 6.

(ITALY)

35. Milan
Antiphoner (pars aestiva); Milan, Bibl. Trivulziana Ms a 14.
36. Rome
Bernhardi Cardinalis et Lateranensis Ecclesiae Prioris Ordo Officiorum Ecclesiae Lateranensis; edited by J. Schlecht (Munich and Freising, 1916).
37. Processional; Rome, Bibl. Vatic. Ms 4750.

(GERMANIC REGIONS)

38. Rheinau (northern Switzerland)
Ordinal; Zürich, Zentralbibliothek, Ms Rheinau 80; edited by A. Hänggi (Freiburg, 1957).

(FRANCE)

39. Laon
Ordinaires de L'église cathédral de Laon; edited by U. Chevalier (*Bibliothèque liturgique* VI, Paris, 1897).
40. Lyons
Ordinal; Paris, Bibl. Nat. lat. Ms 1017.
41. Nevers
Gradual; Paris, Bibl. Nat. nouv. acq. Ms 1235.
42. Prémontré (northern France)
L'Ordinaire de Prémontré d'après des manuscrits du XIIe et du XIIIe siècle (*Bibl. de la revue d'histoire ecclésiastique*, fasc. 22, Louvaine, 1941).

Thirteenth Century

(ENGLAND)

43. Gysburgh (Yorkshire)
Missal-Breviary; British Museum Ms add. 35285; after A. D. 1246.
44. Oxford (?)
Processional-Troper-Proser; Augustinian, St. Frideswide's?; Oxford, Bodleian Ms Lyell 9.
45. Norwich
The Customary of the Cathedral Priory of Norwich; edited by J. Tolhurst as vol. LXXXII (1948) of the Henry Bradshaw Society.
46. Worcester
Antiphoner; Library of the Cathedral, Ms F 160; published in facsimile as vol. XII (1922) of *Paléographie Musicale*.

(FRANCE)

47. Amiens
Ordinaires de l'église Notre Dame d'Amiens par Raoul de Rouvroy; A. D. 1291; edited by Georges Durand (*Mémoires de la soc. des antiquaires de Picardie*, tome 22, Amiens-Paris, 1934).
48. Autun (Burgundy)
Processional; Autun, Bibl. Munic. Ms 183.
49. Bayeux
Ordinaire et coutumier de l'église cathédrale de Bayeux; edited by U. Chevalier (*Bibl. liturgique*, tome VIII, Paris, 1903).

50. Châlons (near Rheims)
Ordinal; Paris, Bibl. Nat. lat. Ms 10579.

51. Chartres
L'Ordinaire chartrain du XIIIe siècle; edited by Yves Delaporte (Chartres, 1953).

52. Compiègne
Ordinal; Paris, Bibl. Nat. lat. Ms 18044.

53. Dijon
Ordinal; edited by Chomton in *Histoire de l'église St-Bénigne de Dijon* (Dijon, 1900).

54. Metz
Processional; St. Arnulph's; Ms 580 of the Cathedral (photographs of this manuscript, which has been destroyed, are at Solesmes).

55. Metz
Ordinal; Paris Bibl. Nat. lat. Ms 990; a notarized seventeenth century copy of the thirteenth century ordinal, Ms 82 of the Cathedral.

56. Rouen
Gradual; Paris, Bibl. Nat. lat. Ms 904; before A. D. 1220; published in facsimile as volume II of *Le Graduel de l'église cathédrale de Rouen au XIIIe siècle* of H. Loriquet (Rouen, 1907).

57. Processional; Rouen Bibl. de la Ville, Ms 222 (A 551).

58. Sens
Ordinal; Paris, Bibl. Nat. lat. Ms 9970.

59. Processional; Sens, Bibl. Munic. Ms 7.

(GERMANIC REGIONS)

60. Münster
Excerpta ex Ordinariis Germanicis; Münster, Bibl. Cap. Ms 4; edited by R. Stapper (Münster, 1936).

(ITALY)

61. Moggio (north-east Italy, near Udine)
Ordinal; Oxford, Bodleian Ms misc. lit. 325.

62. Rome
Gradual; Bibl. Vaticana, Archivo di S. Pietro Ms F. 22.

(LOW COUNTRIES)

63. Douai
Ordinal; Paris, Bibl. nat. lat. Ms 1236.

64. Liège
   Liber Ordinarius Sancti Jacobi Leodiensis; edited by Paul Volk, in
   Beiträge zur Geschichte des alten Monachtums (Münster, 1923).
65. Louvain
   Ordinal; edited by Pl. Lefèvre in *Les Ordinaires de Louvain* (Louvain,
   1960).

Thirteenth-Fourteenth Century

(FRANCE)

66. St. Denis
   Ordinal; Paris, Bibl. Nat. lat. Ms 976.
67. St. Lô (Rouen)
   Ordinal; from a Ms of the Church; Canons Regular; edited in
   Patrologia Latina, CXLVII, 157 ff.
68. Saint-Vasst (Arras)
   Ordinal; Bibl. Munic. of Arras Ms 230 (907); A. D. 1297-1312;
   edited by L. Brou as vols. LXXXVI, LXXXVII (London, 1954-57)
   of the Henry Bradshaw Society.

(SPAIN)

69. Vich (near Barcelona)
   Processional; photographs of this manuscript are at Solesmes; its
   present owner is unknown.

Fourteenth Century

(ENGLAND)

70. Bury St. Edmund's (East Anglia)
   Processional; Norwich Museum, Ms 158. 926. 4g; late fourteenth
   century.
   Paleographical evidence points to a date no earlier than the second
   half of the fourteenth century. This manuscript has no provisions
   for the feast of St. Anne. But another, closely related processional
   (number 82, below) does; and the most likely date in this general
   period for the adoption of the feast is shortly after the decree of
   1383 (see Wilkins, *op. cit.*, III, 178). From this it appears that the
   present manuscript is anterior to this date. The presence of the Transfiguration does not disturb this, for there are at least two other early

English Benedictine appearances, at St. Alban's, Herfordshire, by the second half of the thirteenth century, and at Evesham, by the third quarter of the fourteenth (see *English Benedictine Calendars before* 1100, edited by F. Wormold as vols. LXXVII, LXXXI [London, 1938, 1943-44] of the Henry Bradshaw Society, I, 41; II, 34).

71. Exeter
Ordinale Exoniense; Exeter Chapter Library, Ms 3502; A. D. 1337; ed. J. Dalton as vols. XXXVII, XXXVIII, LXIII (London, 1909, 1926) of the Henry Bradshaw Society.

72. Hereford
Ordinal; British Museum, Ms Harleian 2983.

73. Yorkshire
Processional; church dedicated to St. Oswald; Oxford, Bodleian Ms e. mus. 126.

(FRANCE)

74. Cambrai
Processional; Cambrai, Bibl. Munic. (no number).

75. Verdun
Processional; Verdun Bibl. Munic. Ms 134, Ms 139, Ms 146.

(GERMANIC REGIONS)

76. Essen
Der Liber Ordinarius der Essener Stiftskirche; edited by Franz Arens (Paderborn, 1908).

(ITALY)

77. Dominican Nuns
Processional; Oxford, Bodleian Ms lat. lit. f. 10.

78. Dominican (Aquilea)
Processional; Oxford, Bodleian Ms Lyell 72; second quarter of the century.

Fourteenth-Fifteenth Century

(ENGLAND)

79. Sion (Middlesex)
Processional; St. John's College, Cambridge, Ms F 2.

(FRANCE)

80. Coutances (Normandy)
    Ordinal; Paris, Bibl. Nat. lat. Ms 1301.

Fifteenth Century

(ENGLAND)

81. Barking (near London)
    The Ordinal ... of Barking Abbey; Oxford, University College, Ms 169;
    A. D. 1404; edited by J. Tolhurst as vols. LXV, LXVI (London,
    1927-28) of the Henry Bradshaw Society.
82. Castle Acre Priory (Norfolk)
    Processional; Norwich Museum, Ms 158. 926. 4e.
83. Chester
    Processional; Benedictine Nuns of St. Werburgh; Huntington
    Library, San Marino, California, Ms EL 34 B7; the text of this
    processional has been edited by J. W. Legg as vol. XVIII (1899) of the
    publications of the Henry Bradshaw Society.
84. Essex
    Processional; St. Ossith's Church; Oxford, Bodleian Ms Laud misc.
    329.
85. St. Mary's Abbey (York)
    The Ordinal ... of St. Mary's, York; A. D. 1398-1405; edited by L.
    McLachlan and J. Tolhurst as vols. LXXIII, LXXV, LXXXIV
    (London, 1934, 1937, 1949, 1950) of the Henry Bradshaw Society.
86. Sion
    Processional; Brigettine nuns of Sancti Salvatoris; Oxford, St.
    John's College, Ms 167.

(FRANCE)

87. Dominican
    Processional; Cambridge, Fitzwilliam Library, Ms James 42 (cf.
    number 77, 78, 90, 92, 98).
88. Limoges
    Processional; St Michael's; British Museum, Ms Egerton 3272;
    A. D. 1452.
89. Poor Clares (Perpignan)
    Processional; Oxford, Bodleian Ms lat. lit. e. 8; A. D. 1490.

90. Dominican Nuns (Poissy, vicinity of Paris)
Hours Book and Processional; Oxford, Bodleian Ms Rawl. lit. f. 35;
second half of the century.
91. Saint-Florent (Saumur)
Processional; Manchester, Ryland's Library Ms 385.

(GERMANIC REGIONS)

92. Dominican
Processional; British Museum, Ms add. 28214.
93. Dominican Nuns
Processional; Cambridge University Ms addl. 5336.
94. Medingen (north-west Germany, south of Lüneburg)
Processional; Werden and Cistercian, of St. Mary and Mauritius;
Oxford, Bodleian Ms lat. lit. e. 18.
95. St. Gall
Ordinal; St. Gall Stiftsbibliothek Ms 448.
96. Processional; St. Gall Stiftsbibliothek Ms 486.

(ITALY)

97. (Augustinian)
Ritual and Processional; Oxford, Bodleian Ms Canonici lit. 292.
98. Dominican Nuns
Processional; Oxford, Bodleian Ms Canonici lit. 291.
99. Venice (?)
Manual and Processional; Convent of St. Louis the Bishop(?);
Oxford, Bodleian Ms Canonici lit. 308.

(LOW COUNTRIES)

100. (Augustinian Canonesses)
Manual with processions; Manchester, Ryland's Library Ms 100.
101. Fransiscan
Processional; Ms (no number) of St. Paul's, London; A. D. 1497.
102. Park Abbey (Louvain)
Processional; Oxford, Bodleian Ms liturg. 405; second half of the
century.

Fifteenth (Sixteenth?) Century

(FRANCE)

103. Poor Clares

Processional; Oxford, Bodleian Ms Buchanan e. 20.

104. Autun (south-west of Dijon)

Processional; Autun Bibl. Munic. Ms 98 S, Ms 181 S.

105. Dominican Nuns (Poissy)

Processional-Troper; Cambridge, Fitzwilliam Library, Ms McClean 63.

106. Processional; Stonyhurst College Ms 78.

VI. A HISTORY OF THE OCCASIONS
1. PRE-CHRISTIAN ORIGINS, ROGATION PROCESSIONS, PROCESSIONS BEFORE MASS

The history of the processions of Sarum begins long before the founding of the See in 1075. They, like the Sarum Use as a whole, were for the most part the common practice of the Western Church. The definitive shape of this practice was Roman, but it had roots in the primitive Church, and even in biblical and pagan antiquity.

The early Christians seem to have taken up processions as soon as such public demonstrations were tolerated by the civil authorities. A procession in Milan was mentioned by St. Ambrose in the year 388,[1] and processions in Jerusalem about the same time by Etheria;[2] and in both cities the practice was already established.[3] It is not surprising that they should be taken up quickly. The early Christians inherited a taste for processions from their pagan forbears, and found sanction for them in Scripture.

If justification was found in the biblical processions before the Ark[4] or to the Temple[5] only one Christian procession, Palm Sunday's, can be said really to derive from Scripture.[6] In this respect the more immediate pagan practices had a greater influence. It is not far from the pagan triumphs in which torches were carried, images borne, incense burned and hymns of praise sung on the way to the Capitol,[7] to the processions

---

[1] Letter to Theodosius, in *Patrologia Latina* (PL), XVI, 1107.

[2] A Spanish abbess or nun who wrote an account of the liturgical practice of Jerusalem. This account, part of her *Peregrinatio*, has been edited by L. Duchesne in *Origines du culte chrétien* (fifth edition, Paris, 1925), 512 ff.

[3] Ambrose speaks (*loc. cit.*) of monks, "psalmos canentes ex consuetudine usuque veteri pergebant ad celebritatem Machabaeorum martyrum" (singing psalms after the ancient use and custom as they proceded to the festival in honour of the Machabean Martyrs). At first sight this seems ambiguous, but he would not point out to Theodosius that psalm singing was an old custom.

[4] Joshua VI, 13; I Chronicles, XIII, 7-8.

[5] II Chronicles, XX, 33; II Samuel, VI, 4-5, etc.

[6] Matthew, XXI, 6-12.

[7] See "Triomphes" in *Dictionnaire des antiquités grecques et romaines* (ed. E. Saglio, Paris, 1875-1912); there is record of a triumph (Honorius's) as late as A. D. 402.

organized by St. John Chrysostom[1] (c. 347-407) in which lighted candles were carried, silver crosses borne and psalms sung on the way to the Cathedral.[2] And there was a continuity in more than external features.

On the twenty-fifth of April the pagan Romans had held a procession in honour of the goddess Robigo in which prayers were offered to her for the protection of the crops from mildew. The Christian Romans following a custom already well established in the sixth century[3] held a procession, the Major Litany,[4] on the same day, for the same purpose, and even over much the same route.[5]

Similar circumstances surround the Rogation Days. From the fifth century these have been observed in Gaul with processions on the three days preceding Ascension[6] to seek divine protection for the harvest. A pagan observance, the *Ambarvalia*, with similar processions through the fields had been held alternately the seventeenth to the twentieth and the twenty-seventh to the thirtieth of May.[7]

For still another example there is the Purification procession. The old arrangements for it presented a curious anomaly: penitential trappings for a feast day.[8] The pope marched on foot, not as usual on horseback, with bare feet and in black vestments.[9] It has been suggested that the procession and feast were originally distinct, and with support from certain

---

[1] In imitation of similar processions of the Arians.

[2] Sozomen, *Ecclesiastical History*, VIII, 8, in *Patrologia Graeca*, LXVII, 1535-1538.

[3] Gregory the Great refers to it as "solemnitas annuae devotionis" (a solemnity offered annually) (PL, LXXVII, 1329).

[4] "Litania" from "λιτανια," "a supplication," had come by the sixth century to designate in Greek and in Latin the public processions of penance (E. A. Sophocles, *Greek Lexicon of the Roman and Byzantine Periods* [3rd ed., 1887]). "Major" (cf. Gregory [*loc. cit.*]: "letaniam quae *major* ab omnibus appellatur" [the litany which is called "major" by everyone]) is to be understood to mean "the most important." Elsewhere different occasions were designated the "major" litany (see below).

[5] Duchesne, *Origines*, 304 ff. Cf. J. G. Frazer, *The Golden Bough*, (abridged edition, New York, 1940) 655.

[6] W. Scudamore, in *Dictionary of Christian Antiquities* (ed. W. Smith and S. Cheetham, London, 1880), 1809.

[7] D. DeBruyne, "L'Origine des processions de la chandleur et des rogations ...," in *Revue Bénédictine*, XXXIV (1922), 14-26.

[8] That is, in the West; in the East it was an entirely joyous occasion (see Etheria, *ed. cit.*, 519).

[9] Mabillon's *Ordo XI*, 29, *Ordo XII*, 11-12 (*Museum Italicum*, II, 132, 173 in the edition of 1724); *Ordines* of Saint-Amand (ed. Duchesne in *Origines*, 499).

94

medieval authors,[1] that the former was a Christian carry-over from the pagan *Amburbale* or *Lupercalia*.[2] Both were occasions of purification and expiation, and the first at least involved a procession.[3]

Not to labour the point, the religious procession of triumph or supplication was not a Christian invention. What is more, the Christians did not hesitate to adapt to their purposes certain of the pagan institutions of their ancestors.

ROGATION PROCESSIONS

In the first centuries after the Peace of Constantine processions played a conspicuous part in public worship, particularly at times of threatening calamity. Theodosius ordered processions in the year 394 to plead for divine help in his imminent attack on Eugenius and Arbogast.[4] St. John Chrysostom mentioned litanies held in April of 399 when heavy rains were endangering the harvest.[5] Mamertus, Bishop of Vienne, instituted processions about the year 470 after an earthquake and the destruction of

---

[1] Chiefly Bede (*De Temporum Ratione* [A.D. 725] XII):

Id ipsum [the Purification procession]... eiusdem beatae matris et perpetuae virginis festivitatibus agere... non utique in lustrationem terrestris emperii quinquennem, sed in perennem regni caelestis memoriam. (PL, XC, 351);	This [procession] of our Blessed Mother ever virgin is held on [her] feast, not only with the quinquennial lustration of the Empire, but yearly, in memory of the Queen of Heaven.

and the anonymous author of a sermon (ed. deBruyne, *op.cit.*) in a Corbie manuscript of the tenth century (now Paris, Bibl. Nat. lat. Ms 18296):

Amburbale dicebant ab ambitu urbis... et hoc pro pace petenda faciebant in quinto anno. Quam solempnitatem singulis annis transtulimus in honorem beatae mariae quarto nonas februari.	The Amburbale is so called from the ambulation through the city, and it takes place every five years to pray for peace. This solemnity we have taken over as an annual event on the second day of February in honour of the blessed Mary.

[2] The exponents and arguments for both origins are set out by deBruyne (*op. cit.*); see also F. Holweck under "Candlemas" in the *Catholic Encyclopedia* (16 vols., New York, 1907-14). That either was the specific source for the Candlemas procession cannot be shown conclusively.

[3] See the entries in *A Dictionary of Classical Antiquities* (ed. O. Seyffert, 5th edition, London, 1899).

[4] Rufinus of Aquileia, *Historia Ecclesiastica*, II, 33 in PL, XXI, 539.

[5] *Patrologia Graeca*, LVI, 265.

the royal palace by lightning.[1] Childebert (d. 558), the third son of Clovis, ordered them during his siege of Sargossa.[2] Others in the face of impending disaster are reported for Rheims in 546,[3] for Limoges about 580,[4] for Sicily in 601[5] and for Rome in 590 and 603.[6]

Processions of this kind were frequent enough that Justinian in 527 found it necessary to lay down regulations for them.[7] They remained customary throughout the middle ages, and survived to be provided for in the *Rituale Romanum* of 1614.

Mamertus made the Rogations[8] of 470 a regular observance in his diocese on the three days preceding Ascension. Later,[9] annual proces-

---

[1] Gregory of Tours, *Historia Francorum*, II, 34 in PL, LXXI, 231-232. It may be inferred from chapter IX, 6 that Mamertus' Rogation Days did involve processions. See also Fortunatus' *Vita Germanii* in PL, LXXXVIII, 465. Rogations of three days duration were customary in Gaul even for sudden emergencies; cf. Angilbert's *ordo*, XI (*Qualiter pro tribulatione cruces sequi debeant*), number 2 of the sources, page 326.

[2] Gregory of Tours, *Historia Francorum*, III, in PL LXXI, 263.

[3] Gregory of Tours, *Liber de Gloria Confessorum*, LXXIX, in PL, LXXI, 885-886.

[4] Gregory of Tours, *Vita Sancti Aridii*, VIII, in PL, LXXI, 1124.

[5] Pope Gregory I, *Registrum Epistolarum*, XI, 31, ed. P. Ewald, and M. Hartmann (for *Monumenta Germaniae Historica* [Hanover, 1826-   ]) in 2 vols. (1891, 1899), II, 301.

[6] Gregory of Tours, *Historia Francorum*, X, 1, in PL, LXXI, 528-529; Gregory the Great, *Registrum Epistolarum*, XIII, 2, *ed. cit.*, II, 367.

[7] "Omnibus autem laicis interdicimus ne supplicationes publicas peragant sine religiosissimis episcopis et qui sub eis sunt reverendissimis clericis... sed et venerabiles cruces cum quibus sacerdote in supplicationibus ingrediuntur non alibi qual in locis venerabilibus reponuntur." (*Novelae*, CXXIII, 32, ed. R. Schöll and W. Kroll, in vol. III [Berlin, 1928] of *Corpus Juris Civilis*, 617).

We forbid the laity to conduct public processions without the reverend bishops and their reverend assistants in order that the holy crosses carried by the priest in the processions should not be brought to unsuitable places.

"Supplicatio" translates "λιτανια" in the Greek version of the *Novelae*.

[8] "Rogatio" is the latin equivalent of "λιτανια"; cf. can. 16 of the Council of Clovesho (A. D. 747): "litaniae id est rogationes" (Wilkins, *op. cit.*, I, 97). The council in Mayence in 813 spoke of "letania majore" where it is clear from the context that the Rogation Days were meant (Martène, *De Antiquis Ritibus Ecclesiis* [Venice, 1738], III, 518); and the *Portiforium of St. Wulstan*, an Anglo-Saxon book of 1065-66 from Winchester (ed. for the Henry Bradshaw Soc., 2 vols., 1956-7) uses the term in the same way (I, 62).

[9] Sidonius Apollinaris (d. c. 480) wrote that before Mamertus such supplications were infrequent and irregular:

> Erant quidem prius ... vagae, tepentes, infrequentesque atque sic dixerim oscitabundae supplicationes (*Epistolae*, V, 14, in PL, LVIII, 544).

Sidonius was the son-in-law of the Emperor Avitus and a prefect of Rome, and can therefore be supposed to have been familiar with the liturgical practice of that city as well as that of his

sions for the crops and for public penance became the widespread practice. The Rogation Days of Vienne were enjoined upon all Gaul by the Council at Orléans in the year 511.[1] Britain, as it appears from a letter relating Bede's death, followed the Gallican practice.[2] The council at Tours in 567 ordered similar processions for the first of January.[3] In Spain, according to the Council of Gerona in 517, processions were to be held after Pentecost and at sowing time at the beginning of November.[4] Isidore speaks of them also at the autumnal equinox.[5] In Milan processions were held on Monday, Tuesday and Wednesday following Ascension.[6] In Rome, it will be remembered, there was the Major Litany on St. Mark's Day. Two of these occasions came to be generally accepted.

The Roman observance of an annual rogation procession on the twenty-fifth of April had at first no general currency. Later, however, as part of the movement toward a uniform liturgical practice based on the Roman Rite, it was imposed gradually on the whole of the West. The Council of Clovesho ordered the Roman practice for Britain in 747.[7] The Major Litany entered the Frankish regions with the Roman books in the course of the eighth century[8] but it was not immediately observed. Angilbert's *ordo* omits it;[9] and Amalarius, writing in 812, stressed the

own province. For this reason his statement above and the way he insists on the originality of Mamertus' institution ("invenit, instituit, invexit") suggest that the Major Litany was not yet established in Rome.

[1] Can. 27 (acts ed. by F. Maassen, *Concilia Aeve Merovingici*, for *Monumenta Germaniae Historica* [1893], p. 165 ff.).

[2] Bede died on the day before Ascension, 735.
Concerning this day the letter reads:

A tercia autem hora, ambulavimus cum reliquiis sanctorum ut consuetudo illius diei poscebat (C. Plummer, *Bedae Opera Historica* [Oxford, 1896] I, clxii).	However, at the third hour we walked in procession with the relics of the saints as the customs for that day required.

[3] Maassen, *op. cit.*, 126-7.

[4] Can. 2, 3, H. Bruns, *Canones Apostolarum et Conciliorum* (1893), II, 18 ff.; Isidore, *De Ecclesiasticis Officiis*, I, 40, in PL, LXXXIII, 774.

[5] *Ibid.*, I, 39.

[6] Martène, *op. cit.*, III, 534; cf. number 60 in the sources, fol. 32v, 38v, 44.

[7] Can. 16: "Ut litaniae … agantur … die septimo kalendarum Maiarum, iuxte ritum Romanae Ecclesiae (*loc. cit.*).

[8] It appears in both the Gelasian and Gregorian Sacramentaries, in the Mont-Blandin Gradual (number 3 of the sources) and in the others of the new Roman type.

[9] The surviving fragment (number 2 in the sources) is concerned with just this period of the year.

difference between the Roman and the Gallican practice.[1] In 836 the second council of Aachen ordered the Roman litany for the whole of the Empire.[2]

The Major Litany did not supplant the Rogation Days; it was taken up in addition.[3] This double observance was adopted in Rome during the pontificate of Leo III[4] (795-816), and so became firmly established as part of the official Roman Use.

MASS PROCESSIONS

While rogation processions did customarily terminate with Mass,[5] they stand apart in having been integral, essential features of the liturgy. The processions now to be considered were accessory only. Although it came later to be obscured, they had originally a practical purpose. They served to conduct the celebrant and his ministers to the site of the service.

As early as the middle of the second century the site of a saint's martyrdom or burial was considered especially sanctified to his cult and was the ideal location for the principal celebration of the local Christian community on his feast day.[6] When after the end of the persecutions

---

[1] *De Letania Majore*

Hoc est ieiunium triduanum in vigilia ascensionis Domini ... Romana consuetudo unum diem, id est septimo kalendas maii interponit, quem vocat "in letania majore." (*De Ordine Antiphonarii*, in *Opera omnia Liturgica*, ed. J. M. Hanssens as vols. CXXXVIII-CXL [1948-1950] of *Studi e Testi* [Rome, 1900-], II, 178).

This is the three-day fast on the vigil of Ascension. The Roman usage substitutes a single day, the twenty-fifth of April, and calls it the "major litany."

[2] Can. 10, Mansi, *Sacrorum Conciliorum ... Collectio* (31 vols., 1758-1798), XIV, 678.

[3] From the abstract of the Council of Clovesho: 16mo, ut Rogationum dies et minorum et majorum non omittantur (Sixteenthly, that the Rogation Days, both major and minor, should not be omitted). (A. Hadden, W. Stubbs, *Council and Ecclesiastical Documents*, III [1871], 361). As though a sign of the precedence of the Roman use the term "litania minore" or its plural came to be used for the Rogation Days (see above, p. 94, n. 4).

[4] *Liber Pontificalis*, ed. L. Duchesne (in 2 vols., Bibliothèque des écoles françaises d'Athènes et de Rome, 2e sér. iii, [1886-1892]), II, 12.

[5] Fortunatus' *Vita Germani* (*loc. cit.*) makes it clear that this was also the early practice.

[6] Consider the following passage from the *Martyrdom of Polycarp* (d. 155 or 156 A. D.):

Nous avons recueilli ses ossements plus rares que l'or et plus précieux que les pierres de grand prix. Nous les avons déposés au lieu qui convenait. Que le Seigneur nous donne de nous retrouver là, quand nous le pourrons ... pour célébrer le jour anniversaire de son martyre (translated by P. Jounel in *L'Eglise en prière* [ed. A. Martimort, Paris, 1961], 768). See also St. Jerome's *Vita Hilarionis* (d. 371), in PL, XXIII, 45.

churches were built over or near such places and to house important relics,[1] it was customary for the local bishop or abbot to preside in them at especially solemn celebrations. This occurred not only on the feasts of the saints whose shrines they were but for the more important churches even on the anniversaries of the dedication.[2] From Etheria in the fourth century we learn of processions in which the bishop made his way to celebrations and commemorations in churches built over the holy places of Jerusalem.[3] There is no reason why similar processions should not have been widespread.

In Rome the episcopal Mass was celebrated away from the Cathedral especially frequently. The Liber Pontificalis mentions a circuit of stations in the reign of Pope Hilary (461-468).[4] If it was not so in Hilary's time this circuit, as it was enlarged by successive popes, became something more than a round of the local *martyria* for their respective anniversaries. Fifty-nine station days are specified in the earliest surviving list from about the beginning of the seventh century.[5] The Gregorian Sacramentary, which represents the practice of about the end of the eighth century, lists sixty-eight.[6] Later manuscripts bring the total to eighty-four,[7] including all the Marian feasts, Christmas, Epiphany, Septuagesima, Sexagesima and Quinquagesima Sundays, all the Sundays and weekdays of Lent, Easter and Pentecost and all the days of their octaves, the Sundays of Advent, and the Ember Days. Only a very few of these

---

[1] Before the end of Constantine's rule (d. 337) the basilicas of Holy Sepulchre and Golgotha had been built in Jerusalem; and in Rome, a shrine over the tomb of St. Lawrence and the basilica of the Holy Cross to house the newly recovered relics of the Passion (P. Salmon in *L'Eglise en prière*, 768; F. L. Cross, *Oxford Dictionary of the Christian Church* [ODCC], 790, 1179).

[2] *Peregrinatio, ed. cit.*, 541-2.

[3] *Ibid.*, 516, 528, 530, 536.

[4] *Ed. cit.*, I, 244: "In urbe vero Roma constituit ministeria qui circuirent constitutas stationes" (In the city of Rome he established a ministry to make a circuit of the appointed stations). Tertulian (d. c. 220) used the word "statio" to signify the assembly of the people for a service. By the fifth century it was used in a special sense to designate the assemblies at which the pope presided (see "Statio" in *Glossarium ... Mediae et Infimae Latinitatis* [1678] of Charles DuCange).

[5] Würzburg University Ms Mp. th. fol. 62 (sic), ed. G. Morin, "Le Plus ancien *comes* de l'église romaine," in *Revue Bénédictine*, XXVII (1910), 41-74.

[6] Ed. H. A. Wilson as vol. XLIX (London, 1915) of the Henry Bradshaw Society.

[7] ODCC, 1288. The actual number of station days was certainly much higher, for one can suppose with Duchesne that in the books, "on n'a pas jugé nécessaire de dire où est la station le jour de saint Marcel, de sainte Agnès, de saint Sylvestre, etc.," but that, "le nom du saint ... désigne par luimême l'église où a lieu la fête (*Origines*, 128)."

stations took place at the Arch-Cathedral, St. John's Lateran.[1] The others were distributed among all the great churches of the city.

The locations of some of the stations, for example that at Santa Maria Maggiore on Christmas[2] and that at Santa Croce in Gerusaleme on Good Friday,[3] were clearly chosen for being especially appropriate to the occasion. But most of the stations could have been held just as acceptably —with respect to the liturgy—as well in one church as another. The Roman arrangement was made necessary by that city's growing Christian population. The episcopal Mass attended by the whole Christian community had been a primitive ideal of the Church.[4] The stational Masses in Rome served as a substitute for this ideal. They were another way of maintaining unity in a Christian body grown too large to meet in any one place. The pope made his way to these stations in solemn processions which due to their frequency[5] were a very prominent feature of the Roman liturgy. They remained so at least until the exile of the popes in Avignon.[6]

It is not until the eighth century that there is any substantial record of the general processional practice of the West. From Bede, in his *De Temporum Ratione*, we learn that the Candlemas procession was universal by the year 725, and that processions for the other Marian feasts were gaining ground.[7] Some of the earliest continental service books of the period

---

[1] The Roman sources named above specify the stational churches.

[2] Christ's crib was numbered among the relics of the Basilica, which was known in the early Middle Ages as Santa Maria ad Praesepium.

[3] See page p. 99, n. 1.

[4] St. Ignatius of Antioch (c. 35-c. 107 A. D.), letter to the Ephesians, 5, 2; to the Smyrnians, 8; to the Philadelphians (Alashehr), 4 (J. B. Lightfoot, *The Apostolic Fathers* [3 vols., London, 1885], II, 42, 308, 257).

[5] Duchesne (*Origines*, 128) believed that a procession preceded only those few stations for which a *collectio*, or assembly point, was indicated in the Roman books. It is made clear, however, that on most of the station days there were processions ("ipsius diei [Christmas] quam omnium dominicorum dierum vel paschalium, seu natalicia sanctorum"). Public processions were possibly omitted on some of the weekdays of Lent. The earliest descriptions mention only those of the Wednesdays and Fridays up to Holy Week. The starting point was always the Lateran, even if some of the participants fell in only on the way to the stational church. (See *ordo* XV of the *Ordines Romani*, ed. M. Andrieu for *Specilegium Sacrum Louvaniense* [5 vols., Louvain, 1931-1961], III, 97, 115).

[6] See "Stazione Liturgica" in *Enciclopedia Cattolica* (ed. P. Paschini with others, 12 vols., 1949-1954).

[7] In mense eodem [February], die sanctae Mariae, plebs universa, cum sacerdotibus ac ministris, hymnis modulatae vocis per eccle-

In the month [of February], on Holy Mary's Day, all the people, priests and ministers, singing hymns, march through the churches

from about the end of the eighth century to the end of the ninth[1] contain evidence of other processions. The contents vary. The graduals from Mont-Blandin and Corbie contain processional chants only for Purification and for Ash Wednesday.[2] The Laon Gradual includes, as well, pieces for Palm Sunday. The Senlis Gradual adds others for the lenten ferials[3] and for unspecified saints' days.[4] The Gradual of Compiègne includes all these and chants for Easter. Still, it provides for only five processions in all.

It may seem from these books that processions were generally infrequent. But the Graduals are primarily for the Mass and cannot be safely trusted to indicate them all. Angilbert's *ordo* for St. Riquier,[5] written about the end of the eighth century, describes a fuller practice and one more in keeping with Bede's comments. Mentioned in the surviving fragment are processions for Christmas, Purification, Palm Sunday, Easter, Pentecost, Assumption, Nativity, and feasts of all saints with local shrines. What the *ordo* calls for, as far as it goes, is processions for all the major feasts and Sundays. It seems safe then to assume that at least Epiphany and Annunciation would be included in this list if the document were intact; and Ash Wednesday, since this procession is so well documented.

The surviving graduals from the tenth and eleventh centuries present much the same picture as the earlier ones, and leave a great many questions unanswered. But there are enough books which specifically prescribe processions for the major festivals[6] and Sundays, and for Ash Wednesday, to make it clear that these were widespread in this period

---

sias perque congrua urbis loca procedit, datosque a pontifice cuncti cereos in manibus gestant ardentes; et augescente bona consuetudine, id ipsum in caeteris quoque eiusdem beatae matris et perpetuae virginis festivitatibus agere (*loc. cit.*, p. 95, n. 1).

and the neighbouring parts of the city, carrying lighted candles given them by the pope, and it is a growing and good custom to do the same for the other feasts of the Blessed Mother ever virgin.

[1] Sources 3 through 8.

[2] The rogation processions are left out of account in this discussion.

[3] "Incipiunt antiphonas de ieiuniorum diebus a feria quarta caput de ieniuiis.".

[4] "De natalitiis sanctorum."   [5] Number 2 of the sources.

[6] The Calendar and the rank assigned to feasts have always varied locally. This means, for example, that at Rheinau, Laon, Louvain, and Münster Christmas was not counted among the feasts which rated a procession (see numbers 38, 39, 65, 60 in the sources). Similar variation existed in the solemnity of the celebration of certain octaves, so that there was never a uniform practice for the days of Easter and Pentecost weeks.

if they were not general.[1] Processions for the weekdays of Lent were probably more common than they appear to have been; as they use Ash Wednesday pieces they do not require an entry in the service books. The later practice for these lenten processions was not, by the way, everywhere the same. They were usually held, as at Sarum, on Wednesdays and Fridays,[2] excepting Holy Week and any day a feast was celebrated. But in some churches they were extended to the Mondays of Lent.[3] A few ordinals call for similar processions in Advent,[4] and even during the summer period.[5]

One thing is sure about these early centuries; and that is that processions were becoming more and more frequent. Bede remarked on this at the beginning of the eighth century; and for confirmation later one has only to compare the Anglo-Saxon and Norman ordinals for Canterbury.[6]

In the local liturgies the procession commonly played a part comparable in importance and even similar in detail to its role in Rome. But although processions were natural enough in Rome, where they were prompted by the circumstances of the city's ceremonial, in most local situations they were unnecessary and awkwardly arranged.

In some centres[7] a number of the processions did keep their primitive function. They served to conduct the local bishop or abbot, or his representative,[8] to stations in parish churches on certain feasts and Sundays. In most of these cases, however, it could be argued that the whole arrangement was extraneous. Except for rogation days, which

---

[1] To speak of the general practice is not to include the special case of certain austere monastic orders. The Dominicans had very few processions, only for the greatest occasions. The Rule of the Franciscans allowed only two processions, for Palm Sunday and for Purification. The Cistercians were allowed only those for Candlemas and Ash Wednesday until St. Bernard introduced one for Ascension. But the severity of the *regulae* in this respect was in individual cases often mitigated, especially in the later middle ages (see the sources; S. J. P. VanDijk and J. Walker, *The Origins of the Modern Roman Liturgy* (London, 1960, 391 ff.).

[2] Cf. page 100, note 5, above.

[3] Cf. page 99.

[4] Bury St. Edmund's, Canterbury (sources 82, 20).

[5] Dijon (Martène, *op. cit.*, IV, 806), Anglo-Saxon Benedictine Houses (source 9).

[6] Sources 9, 20.

[7] Amiens, Bayeux, Chartres, Cluny, Münster, Rheinau, etc. (numbers 47, 49, 51, 21, 60, 38 in the sources).

[8] In later times the bishop was not always present in the Mass procession. However, all the early descriptions show it to have been an episcopal solemnity. In Rome the stational procession (but not the station) was omitted when the pope was absent (VanDijk, *op. cit.*, 170).

traditionally united the whole community in a common petition and—what were almost as rare in smaller centres—feasts of saints with local shrines, there could be little advantage, liturgical or practical, for a bishop or abbot to celebrate Mass away from his own church. In small cities like Chartres or Rheinau frequent station days could not have been prompted by the same considerations as in Rome.

Usually stational Masses were infrequent and account for only a small proportion of the local processions.[1] To be sure, there was always some ostensible purpose; processions were never aimless wanderings. But most performed no necessary action. What at first sight appears to be their immediate prompting is usually only a pretext to accommodate them. Consider, for example, that in some places[2] the participants walked in silence, and without ceremony to a neighbouring church—where the blessing was read over the palms or candles or the final morning office recited—and began there a procession back to Mass in their own. According to another arrangement the procession set out from its own choir to another church for a brief commemoration and returned immediately for Mass.[3] The most frequent arrangement everywhere had processions follow a circuitous route entirely within the church or church grounds, pausing for remembrances at church fixtures.

These circumstances surrounding the performance of the processions give us every reason to believe that the practices were not indigenous.

The pre-eminence of Rome had given its liturgy authority even when the province of the Roman Rite was still very restricted. Early records of episcopal stations and solemn processions in Milan and Tours[4] suggest that they, as perhaps other cities, owed something for such observances to the Station Days of Rome. Such a debt in later times can scarcely be doubted. Beginning about the seventh century, the Roman Rite was exported widely. By the eleventh it had displaced the provincial rites in almost all of the churches of Latin Christendom. Bearing in mind that all of the medieval uses, including Sarum's, were in most other

---

[1] A stational Mass in another church was usual for all rogation days and was very often the case for Palm Sunday. As for processions to Mass in neighbouring churches on the feasts of their patrons or on the anniversaries of their dedication, in practice they were not the rule. Consider, for example, that the official Sarum rite made no provisions for them.

[2] St. Riquier, Anglo-Saxon Benedictine Houses, Bayeux, Essen (number 2, [p. 321], 9 [p. 31], 49 [p. 118-119], 76 [p. 4]).

[3] Anglo-Saxon Benedictine Houses (number 9, p. 32-33), Chartres (number 51, p. 76).

[4] St. Ambrose, letter to Theodosius, in PL, XVI, 1107; Gregory of Tours, *Historia Francorum*, V, 4, 11, in PL, LXXI, 320, 325.

respects only local variations of the Roman Rite, the origin of the processional customs is clear enough. In the case of three of the Marian feasts there is also more concrete evidence of Roman influence.

From Bede—to return to his comments in *De Temporum Ratione*[1]—we learned that processions for the Annunciation, the Assumption and the Nativity had only just started to become customary in 725. The Liber Pontificalis records that these processions had been instituted only a few years before in Rome by Sergius I, Pope from 687 to 701.[2] This innovation[3] would have been reported in Britain by the many people Bede says were travelling to Rome.[4]

Processions for ordinary Sundays seem not to have been general before the twelfth century. None of the earliest of our sources specify them,[5] nor do many of the books from the tenth and eleventh centuries.[6] The significance of this silence is attested to by the clear practice of a few

---

[1] See page 95.

[2] *Ed. cit.*, I, 376.

[3] Sergius is credited (*loc. cit.*) also with the Purification procession:

Constituit autem ut diebus adnuntiationis Domini, Dormitionis [Assumption], Nativitatis sanctae Dei Genetricis semperque virginis Mariae ac asncti Symeonis quod Ypanti Greci appellant [Purification], letania exeat a sancto Hadriano et ad sanctam Mariam pupulus occurrat.	Moreover, he decreed that on Annunciation, Assumption, Nativity and Candlemas the procession will set out from St. Hadrian's and join with the people at St. Mary's.

But the characteristic procession was certainly much older (see below). Sergius would simply have adapted it to the stational procession.

[4] *Historia Anglorum*, V. 7 (PL, XCV, 238):

At this period [c. 688-c. 731] many English people followed this custom [visiting Rome], both noble and simple, layfolk and clergy, men and women alike.	His temporibus plures de gente anglorum, nobiles, ignobiles, laici, clerici, viri ac feminae certatim facere consuerunt.

Historia Anglorum, V. 19 (PL, XCV, 263):

[Bishop Wilfrid] decided to visit Rome and see what ecclesiastical and monastic customs were in use at the apostolic see.	Proposuitque animo venire Roma, et qui ad sedem apostolicam ritus ecclesiastici sive monasteriales servarentur, videre.

[5] Unless Sundays were among the unspecified occasions" ad cruces [deducendas]" (see below, chapter VIII) at Senlis (number 6, p. 211); this rubric occurs also in the Mont-Rénaud codex (number 12, p. 45 v), and almost totally effaced in the Chartres Gradual (number 10, p. 129).

[6] Sunday processions are indicated in number 10, 16, 17, 19, 23, 24, 27, 29 of the sources.

churches whose only regular dominical procession in the tenth and eleventh centuries was that of the priest for the *Asperges*.[1]

The station days in Rome never included all Sundays. The increase in the number of the processions was not owing to any corresponding change in the Roman customs. Rather, it was due to a change in the conception of the processions. Outside Rome they seldom served any real purpose. The procession came to be regarded as a ceremonial embellishment of the liturgy. With the growing importance attached to the observance of Sundays bringing enforced abstention from work and obligatory attendance at Mass,[2] it was only natural that more and more churches should extend to them all the trappings of the great feasts. But a procession to another church would have been too inconvenient to repeat weekly; not, however, one which followed the easy, sheltered course of the *Asperges*.

Although exorcised water is mentioned in connection with the dedication of former pagan temples by popes Vigilius (538-555) and Gregory I (590-604),[3] its use as a regular dominical observance became universal much more recently. The *Asperges* appears first about the beginning of the ninth century as a monastic practice in the "Supplement of Alcuin" to the Gelasian Sacramentary.[4] In 847 by a decree of Leo IV[5] it was ordered for the whole Church; but the rite may have spread only slowly. It was known soon after in Rheims and about the end of the century in the St. Riquier *ordo*.[6] But it appears in none other of our sources before the tenth century.

At Sarum the *Asperges* proper took place within the choir. Commonly however, it included a tour of the church before Mass by the celebrant for the purpose of sprinkling the people with Holy Water.[7] It was surely

[1] Anglo-Saxon Benedictine Houses, Canterbury under the Normans (number 8, 19 in the sources); the Sunday processions mentioned in the St. Riquier *ordo* (number 2, p. 327) would be of this same kind.

[2] ODCC, 1305.

[3] Letter to Profuturus, Bishop of Braga, in PL, LXXXIV, 832; "Dialogues," III, 30, in PL, LXXVII, 228.

[4] Ed. H. A. Wilson (Oxford, 1894), 223-225.

[5] Philippe Labbe, *Sacrosancta Concilia ad Regiam Editionem Exacta* (1671-1673), VIII, 37.

[6] It is referred to by Bishop Hincmar (elected 845) in his *Epistola Synodica*, cap. 5 (Labbe, *op. cit.*, VIII, 570; Angilbert's *ordo* mentions "aqua benedicta", and (presumably) the *Asperges* procession (number 2 in the sources, p. 324, 327).

[7] There was frequently a more extensive ceremony than required by Pope Leo's decree, especially in the monasteries. At Cluny, for example, the priest sprinkled Holy Water in the infirmary, the dormitory, the refectory and the storehouse (number 21, p. 654). At Sarum,

this which suggested the similar course followed everywhere for the processions on ordinary Sundays.

This circumscribed route, although frequently extended somewhat to include the cloister or the churchyard—in keeping with the greater solemnity of the occasions—was used widely even for festivals, and frequently, as at Sarum, for all the processions. It is likely, however, that this came about only later, and that at first more imposing arrangements were the rule. This was the case at Canterbury. The earlier practice there had been to hold the Candlemas procession from a nearby parish church back to St. Augustine's. After the Conquest Lanfranc directed that the same procession was to be held within the conventual church.[1]

Even where the outdoor procession held ground for certain occasions the Sunday version was frequently called for in case of bad weather.

it will be remembered, the people were sprinkled first, from the choir; the altars later as the priest passed them in the procession; and the cemetery after the procession had returned to the choir.

[1] Cf. number 9 and number 20 of the sources.

VII. A HISTORY OF THE OCCASIONS
2. PROCESSIONS AT VESPERS, MATINS, AND FOR SPECIAL CEREMONIES

Simpler commemorations as well as Masses were often held at special sites. It is clear from the Gregorian Sacramentary that the pope presided at Vespers on some of the great feasts[1] and that the office was held in the appropriate Roman churches.[2] The procession to the Vespers station at Santa Maria Maggiore for the feast of the Assumption is described in one of the *Ordines Romani*.[3] There must have been others like it for similar occasions.

In Jerusalem, among those seen by Etheria in the fourth century were processions held regularly after Vespers from the main church to the sanctuary which housed Christ's Cross.[4] Amalarius in 812 knew of short offices in Rome, held "at various altars," "at the cross," and "at the font."[5]

Amalarius seems to have known of no such practices outside of Rome, but later, processions at Vespers to altars, to the rood and to the font were widespread in the West.

To the font and crucifix.—Beginning with the earliest books virtually all ordinals call for such processions after Vespers during the week after Easter and Pentecost. These same observances may have been known in Rome in very early times. They are provided for in the Gelasian Sacramentary[6] and in the *Ordines*[7].

We have seen at Sarum that the commemorations at the rood continued with processions at first Vespers of the Sundays after Easter. These seem

---

[1] Consider the prayers "ad vesperos" (*ed. cit.*, 14, 28, 85, 88, 112). There can be no doubt that the Sacramentary was intended for the use of the pope (see Duchesne, *Origines*, 129).

[2] Cf. the rubric, "ad vesperos ubi supra" (*ed. cit.*, 14, 112), that is, in the same church as the stational Mass.

[3] Andrieu, *op. cit.*, V, 359.

[4] *Peregrinatio, ed. cit.*, 514.

[5] "Per diversa altaria diversorum locorum, saepissime tamen ad crucem et ad fontes" (*De Ordine Antiphonarii*, LII, in *PL*, CV, 1295).

[6] Page 72 in the edition of L. C. Mohlberg (Rome, 1960).

[7] Ordo XXVII. XXXb. Andrieu, op. cit., III; 475-477.

to be indicated in some of the earliest books of the Frankish monastic houses,[1] although they cannot be found in England before the Normans.[2] The ancient Roman *ordines* leave no record of such memorials. This and the diversity in their practice suggest a provincial origin. These processions became widespread but they were never general. In some places[3] as at Sarum they were held over most of the year, but elsewhere[4] they occurred only in Paschal time.

To altars of the saints.—In Rome processions after Vespers can be supposed to have been customary to conduct the pope to the "diversa altaria diversorum locorum" for the short offices mentioned by Amalarius.[5] The occasions for these are not given but traces of them seem to survive in the Gregorian Sacramentary. It contains prayers addressed to St. John the Evangelist to be said after Vespers of his feast.[6] The directions, "ad fontem," "ad sanctam Andream," refer to chapels at the Lateran. A similar prayer is included for the Baptist.[7]

Processions at Vespers of saints' feasts to altars dedicated in their honour could be found at St. Riquier in Angilbert's time.[8] They were later widespread, and common especially in France and England, but they never became universal. The usual practice was to hold them as at Sarum, after first Vespers of the feasts, and only to altars[9] within the cathedral or conventual church. In some places,[10] however, processions were made even to altars in other churches.

The processions of the first three nights of Christmas in honour of St. Stephen, St. John and the Holy Innocents probably began as pro-

---

[1] Mainz (number 13, f. 49v), Limoges (number 16, ff. 165v, 176v); they were certainly the practice at Cluny in the eleventh century (number 21).

[2] Number 20 of the sources; the *Regularis Concordia* (number 9), while it mentions other processions at Vespers, makes no mention of these.

[3] Barking, Exeter, Norwich, Rouen, Laon, Chartres, Dijon, Lyons, etc. (numbers 81, 71, 57, 39, 51, 53, 40).

[4] Tynemouth, Yorkshire, Châlons, Coutances, Rome (numbers 32, 73, 50, 80, 36).

[5] *Loc. cit.*

[6] *Ed. cit.*, 14.

[7] *Ibid.*, 85. For the chapels at the Lateran see Andrieu, *op. cit.*, III, 364.

[8] Number 2 of the sources, p. 327-8.

[9] In Rome, at the Lateran, processions to the font at (both) Vespers of St. John, and for certain other occasions, were still customary in the twelfth century (see number 36, p. 13, 15, 4). At Chartres the commemoration after first Vespers of Mary Magdalen was not held at her altar (perhaps there was none), but at the crucifix, whose significance for this saint is obvious (number 51, p. 165).

[10] Châlons, Chartres, Laon, Metz, Norwich, St. Denis, St. Riquier (numbers 50, 51, 39, 54, 45, 66, 2).

cessions of this same kind. In some churches they were included in spite of the fact that the appropriate altars did not all exist. In these cases it is likely that they were adopted for certain special features which had become associated with the occasions. These features will be discussed later.

Some ordinals call for processions to altars for the recitation of the vesperal office itself,[1] or part of it.[2]

PROCESSIONS AT MATINS

Processions at Matins to the crucifix for commemorations of the Cross were common in the churches of England and Normandy, and can be found in the books of some Benedictine houses elsewhere.[3] These ceremonies were held not only in the week following Easter and Pentecost as at Sarum, but in some churches[4] at Sunday Matins as counterparts to the processions at First Vespers.

Similarly, processions at Matins were held in some churches to correspond to the vesperal processions to saints' altars.[5]

Processions in the early morning in remembrance of the journey of the three Marys to Christ's sepulchre had been known in the West as early as the sixth century.[6] However, the only Easter morning procession of any currency, the one with the crucifix as at Sarum, belongs to the ceremonial deposition and elevation of the Cross. This rite from beginnings in the tenth century in Germany spread widely over Europe.[7]

PROCESSIONS FOR THE SPECIAL CEREMONIES OF ASH WEDNESDAY AND HOLY WEEK

For the expulsion and reconciliation of the penitents.—As early as the time of St. Ambrose (d. 397) the Thursday before Easter had been the time for

---

[1] St. Riquier, Cluny (numbers 2, 21).

[2] The last part including the Magnificat at Bayeux (number 49), Strassbourg (Martène, *op. cit.*, III. 512).

[3] Dijon, Münster, Essen, Rheinau (numbers 53, 60, 76, 38).

[4] Rheinau, Laon, Rouen, Bury St. Edmund's, Cluny (numbers 38, 39, 57, 82, 21).

[5] Bury St. Edmund's, Cluny, Rheinau, Laon, St. Denis, St. Mary's (York) (numbers 82, 21, 38, 39, 66, 85 [? see p. 46]).

[6] They are mentioned by St. Caesar of Arles (Migne, *Dictionnaire des Cérémonies* [3 vols., Paris, 1846-47], III, 12).

[7] For the spread of this ceremony see Solange Corbin, *La Déposition liturgique du Christ au vendredi saint* (Paris, 1960); K. Young, *The Drama of the Medieval Church* (2 vols., Oxford, 1933), I, 121-122.

public reconciliation of penitent sinners with the church.[1] Some kind of ceremonial reconciliation on Holy Thursday was known widely in Gaul by the eighth century, for special prayers, apparently Gallican in origin, appear in the Gelasian Sacramentary.[2] The earliest of the purely Roman sources to mention such a ceremony, the *Ordo Romanus Antiquus*,[3] is no older than the tenth century.[4]

The procession of reception[5] to conduct the absolved penitents into the church was general.

The ceremonial expulsion of the sinners from the church on Ash Wednesday was not the practice of the Gelasianum. The first appearance is in the later, probably eleventh-century additions to the above mentioned *Ordo Romanus Antiquus*. In the ordinals there is frequently no mention of any such practice nor, of course, of any procession.[6]

For the stripping and washing of the altars on Holy Thursday.—It seems from a remark of Isidore of Seville that this practice was known widely at an early date.[7] The procession from altar to altar for the ritual washing was the custom in many churches. The time for it varied: it can be found not only after the mid-day meal as at Sarum but also between Tierce and Sext, after Vespers, and at nightfall.

For the Adoration of the Cross on Good Friday. — In Rome it was the custom of the pope, perhaps as early as the first half of the eighth century, to go in procession with his ministers, barefoot, from the Lateran to Santa Croce for the adoration of the Cross.[8] Some form of this ceremony, often involving a procession, was later universal in the Western Church.

For the blessing of the new fire and incense.—The striking of a new fire on Holy Saturday was a custom in Celtic and Gallican regions from at least the sixth century.[9] In Rome in the eighth century it was performed "in loco foras basilica" on each of the three days preceding Easter;[10] but

---

[1] *Epistolae*, 20, 25, in PL, XVL, 1001-2.

[2] *Ed. cit.*, 63. See A. Chavasse, *Le Sacramentaire gélasien* (Tournai, 1958), 147-153.

[3] Appendix I to *ordo* L, Andrieu, *op. cit.*, V, 367.

[4] Duchesne, *Origines*, 458, n. 5.

[5] See below.

[6] Cf. the extracts from various ordinals given by Martène, *op. cit.*, I, 795-818.

[7] *De Ecclesiasticis Officiis*, I, 29, in *PL*, LXXXIII, 764.

[8] *Ordo* XXIII, Andrieu, *op. cit.*, III, 266, 270.

[9] Duchesne, *Origines*, 263-64.

[10] *Ordo* XXVI, Andrieu, *op. cit.*, III, 326.

it was the former, and perhaps older practice[1] which prevailed.

In later times processions were sometimes connected with the rite, depending on the location of the ceremony, "ad portam monasterii," "ad cornu altaris," "ad gradum altaris," "in altari beatae Mariae," and even, "ad aliam ecclesiam."[2]

There is no mention in the earliest sources of the blessing of the incense; but this later came to be attached to the service in many churches.[3]

Processions to the font on the Easter and Pentecost Vigil. — Early references to the consecration of the font in the writings of St. Cyprian, St. Ambrose and many others[4] show that this was a prelude to baptism from apostolic times. The position of the font being fixed, and usually at some distance from the site of most of the liturgy, this procession must be among the oldest everywhere. A description in one of the oldest of the *Ordines Romani*[5] shows that processions in Rome on Easter and Pentecost eve were customary in the sixth or seventh century.

PROCESSIONS OF RECEPTION

Processions for the reception of eminent visitors into the church were provided for everywhere. Such would have been the nature of the procession reported by Bede for the missionary Augustine in 596, and this is by no means the earliest example.[6] In Rome they were customarily held for the pope by the regional clergy when he reached the stational churches.[7]

Locally these processions would be frequently called for. Monasteries everywhere received not only official visits from patrons, visiting abbots, other prelates, and so forth, but also—being bound by the Rule to extend hospitality to strangers—visits from many people ranking up to the highest nobility who used the houses as places of rest in their travels. The ceremonial reception was given as well to the bishop or abbot on his return to his own church from a journey.

---

[1] See Andrieu's introduction to *ordo* XXVI (*loc. cit.*).
[2] Kärnten, Narbonne, Prémontré, Arles, and Auxerre respectively (see the excerpts from the ordinals in Martène, *op. cit.*, III, 406-7).
[3] But not everywhere (*ibid.*, 407).
[4] Martène, *op. cit.*, III, 419.
[5] *Ordo* XI, Andrieu, *op. cit.*, II, 444.
[6] Gevaert notes one for the year 546 (*op. cit.*, 167).
[7] *Ordo* I, Andrieu, *op. cit.*, II, 75-76.

VIII. THE FORM AND CONSTITUTION
OF THE PROCESSIONS

The surviving ordinals and processionals show that throughout the West the processions were similar. They included ordinarily the celebrant, his ministers (for the Mass) and the choir, with Gospel texts, thuribles, candles, crosses and Holy Water. These constituents were to some extent determined by the occasion and by ancient use. Nonetheless, the influence of the Roman customs was great, and is responsible at least for the uniformity of the practice.

A substantial picture of the processions in Rome survives from as early as the eighth century in descriptions which have come to be known as the *Ordines Romani*.[1] These descriptions, written, significantly, for the use of churches outside Rome, were circulated widely. Copies can be found from all over Western Europe.[2] In the ordinary stational procession which they describe the pope set out from the Lateran with his ministers and officials, with candlesticks, a vessel for water, a text of the Gospel and a great many other items, to the stational church. There cross bearers were waiting, and thurifers and cerofers to conduct him to the altar.[3] The papal ceremonial was a great deal more elaborate than the local. But all of the common features of the later general practice were present. Bearing in mind the extent of the Roman influence in other respects it cannot be mistaken here.

At Angilbert's monastery the form of the papal processions was imitated quite closely. His *ordo* requires for St. Riquier the same sevenfold organization as the *Ordines Romani*[4]—a feature which was a result in Rome of representation by each of the city's seven *regiones*. In later times, however, the churches for all ordinary purposes settled upon processions of more modest dimensions.

---

[1] *Ed. cit.*

[2] For a list of the sources see *ibid.*, I.

[3] From *ordo* I (*ibid.*, II, 72 ff.).

[4] Cf. number 2 of the sources (p. 324) with Andrieu's *ordo* I (*loc. cit.*) and the Saint-Amand *ordines* (*ed. cit.*, 494, 500). To this day in the papal chapel, and in the Cathedral of Lyons, seven candelabra are carried to the altar by seven acolytes in the procession before Mass (Martimort, *op. cit.*, 633, n. 1).

First[1] was carried Holy Water. Blessed water is specified in the St. Riquier *ordo* and all those later. Although this was in some places—in a kind of continuation of the *Asperges*—used to sprinkle certain of the church fixtures during the Sunday procession, it was used equally on other days when no such action occurred. The water in the processions may originally have had no connection with the lustration. In the papal procession of *Ordo* I the water vessel is an "aquamanus", i.e. a hand basin,[2] and probably intended for ablutions.

Crosses, one or more, were in almost every case carried next.[3] They are mentioned in the very earliest descriptions of Christian processions. Originally they may have been intended as insignia of the bishop. It must not be forgotten that the procession, especially in the beginning, was an episcopal solemnity. Later, to be preceded by a cross was a privilege restricted to a metropolitan and denied except rarely by special permission to ordinary diocesan bishops. But that is not to say that the earlier use was not freer.[4] Whatever their first meaning, crosses have been used in processions independent of the bishop from at least the beginning of the sixth century.[5]

Quite early, different kinds of crosses were used to indicate the character of the occasions. The one of painted wood required by the Sarum Ordinal for the lenten processions is mentioned in an *ordo* from about the end of the eighth century.[6] The Sarum inventory of 1214-1222[7] lists several others, one a gilded processional cross set with precious stones, doubtless for great occasions, and another, a plainer silver cross for Sundays. Similar entries are common in other medieval inventories.[8]

Frequently, ordinals will call for two crosses in the procession, although sometimes only for the greater feasts. In the later middle ages, when the feasts had been elaborately classified,[9] it was widely customary to indicate

[1] Very often a verger preceded to clear the way, but he formed no real part of the procession.
[2] Andrieu, *op. cit.*, II, 73.
[3] At Sens the practice was exceptional. The cross was carried by the sub-deacon in his usual place (number 54, f. 48v). At Coutances it was carried in this same position, but by a deacon (number 80, f. 10 v).
[4] Bede reports that a cross was borne before Augustine on his entry into Canterbury in the year 597 (PL, XCV, 56). This was before he had been consecrated Archbishop.
[5] See page 96.
[6] From Saint-Amand, *ed. cit.*, 494.
[7] Ed. C. Wordsworth, *Ceremonies and Processions of the Cathedral Church of Salisbury* (Cambridge, 1901), 169 ff.
[8] See "Processional Cross" in the *Catholic Encyclopedia*.
[9] The earliest books differentiate only between double and simple feasts. The distinctions

their rank by carrying three crosses for the first class (principal or major double) feasts, two for the next lower (minor double) class and one for the ordinary (inferior double) feasts and Sundays. For the ferial processions the cross was commonly omitted.

Candles were carried next, and following them, incense. These too had a long history in processions, going back even to pre-Christian times. In later centuries these were merely decorative, carried to add to the solemnity of the occasion. But with the water and the Gospels they may have been intended in the beginning to supplement, and on occasion even provide the necessities for Mass at the site of the station.[1]

Later usage fixed the number of candles or candelabra carried in the procession at two, whatever the occasion. For the incense one thurible sufficed for ordinary feasts and Sundays, but two were the rule for the more important days.

Next in the procession walked the officiants, the subdeacon, the deacon and the priest.[2] Occasionally one finds that as in the modern Roman usage the priest walked with his ministers at the end of the procession.[3] But usually this position was reserved for the bishop or abbot whether or not he was to be the celebrant.

Ordinarily only the sub-deacon carried a text of the Gospel.[4] But for the more important occasions there were often two, the other usually carried by the deacon .

Following walked the monks or clerks, those of highest rank last except for the choir rulers who walked just behind the priest, probably that they might better lead the singing.

In late medieval times the usual vestments of the bearers of the Holy Water, crosses, candles and incense were albs or surplices. The priest and his ministers vested for the Mass, the celebrant, in addition, wearing a

---

"principal," "major" and so on don't appear at Sarum before the fourteenth century, although they can be found from the thirteenth elsewhere (see VanDijk, *op. cit.*, 386).

[1] After the procession the candles were set beside the altar (later, on it), and so provided at least part of the light for Mass (ODCC, 40). A text of the Gospels and incense would of course be called for during the service. As for the water, see above, p. 113.

[2] At Coutances there was a deacon (with the cross), two sub-deacons (both with Gospel texts), two more deacons, two priests "revistiti", and four other priests (number 80, f. 10v). The Sarum Processional similarly calls for all the deacons and sub-deacons to walk together whenever the bishop was celebrating. Such a multiplication of ministers may then have been for some special episcopal Mass.

[3] As in the ordinal of the Augustinian Friars (A. D. 1295), and in the official Franciscan Missal, and at Essen (see VanDijk, *op. cit.*, 295, 391-2; number 76 of the sources p. 9).

[4] At Sens the deacon carried the text (number 58, f. 48v).

cope, usually of silk.[1] Silk copes were sometimes worn by the choir rulers or even by all the choir depending on the rank of the day. Otherwise the ordinary copes of the habit were the rule. The bishop wore his pontificals.

There were certain other occasional features of the processions. Bare feet, ashes and sackcloth were common signs of penance. The carrying of banners at the head of the procession was widespread, but restricted usually to great occasions.[2] The special standards, "Lion" and "Dragon" used symbolically in churches following the Sarum Rite for the Rogation Days, and the hair-cloth banner used on Ash Wednesday and Holy Thursday were not general.[3] Occasionally one finds that other "ornamenta mobilia,"[4] objects such as the image of the Blessed Virgin,[5] were carried in the procession on great feasts. Relics were customary for rogation days from at least the sixth century[6] and were carried on occasion in other processions too, especially on Palm Sunday, but there was no uniform practice. The reliquary occupied a position in the procession in front of the sub-deacon.

Certain processions had special features. For the Purification the whole choir—and the people when the procession was public—carried lighted candles. The origin of this custom is obscure. It was perhaps first a pagan practice. Cyril of Scythopolis noted it in the East as early as the sixth century.[7] In the West the candles are mentioned practically from the first appearance of the feast.[8]

The carrying of Palm leaves in a procession on the Sunday before Easter was very early a custom in Jerusalem. Etheria described it there

---

[1] At least later when it was available. In Toulouse in the twelfth century a wool festal cope was called for (number 34, f. 5v). The cope—or *pluviale*, rain-cape, as it was sometimes called—is a sure sign that the processions were intended to be outdoors, however seldom this might have been the case in later times. For the cope see E. Bishop, *op. cit.*, 260 ff.

[2] At Essen there seem to have been banners even for ordinary Sundays (number 76, p. 9).

[3] A dragon-standard does seem to have been carried also in Italy for rogation processions (see Caxton's translation of the *Golden Legend* (*Lombardica Historia*), ed. F. S. Ellis for Temple Classics [7 vols., 1900], I, 105; this is mentioned also by Pellicia [1780] quoted by Cheetham, *op. cit.*, I, 579).

[4] Cluny (number 21, p. 656), Rheinau (number 38, p. 33).

[5] St. Mary's (York) (number 85, p. 94).

[6] Gregory of Tours mentions them in Limoges in the year 580. See page 96.

[7] Life of Abbot Theodosius, ed. E. Schwartz, in *Texte und Untersuchungen zur Geschichte der altchristlichen Literatur* (Leipzig, 1882-), XLIX, Hft. 2 (1939), 236.

[8] See Bede, *De Temporum Ratione, ed. cit.*, 351.

in the fourth century[1] and Cyril of Scythopolis again in the sixth.[2] Its way to the West may have been through the close connection between Jerusalem and Spain. Etheria, it will be remembered, was Spanish.[3] It was known in Toledo in the latter part of the seventh century,[4] and possibly even earlier in Seville.[5] By the eighth century the palms appear in Frankish regions. They are mentioned in the Bobbio Missal about the beginning of the century,[6] and later, this time unmistakably in the procession in Angilbert's *ordo* for St. Riquier.[7] One of the manuscripts of the Gregorian Sacramentary includes a prayer for the blessing of the palms, and worded to suggest that they were carried.[8] The prayer is believed to be a Gallican addition and no part of the Roman original. Amalarius about the year 830 could speak of the characteristic procession as well-established.[9] In Rome, however, in the eighth century and perhaps for some centuries following[10], palms seem not to have figured in the Mass.

The Palm Sunday procession was customarily held with more than usual solemnity, often with banners and relics, and almost always out of doors. But until late in the eleventh century the only special feature of any currency was the carrying of palms or branches in the same way as candles were carried for the Purification. There had been no attempt to make the commemoration of Christ's triumph more representative. It was apparently first in England under Lanfranc[11] that it became the practice to carry the Blessed Sacrament to represent the person of Christ.

[1] *Ed. cit.*, 525, 526.

[2] *Life of St. Euthamius*, XI, in *Acta Sanctorum*, II (1643), 668.

[3] For other known ties between Spain and Jerusalem see H. Anglés in the *New Oxford Dictionary of Music* (ed. A. Hughes, Oxford, 1954-), II, 81.

[4] Number 1 of the sources.

[5] Isidore speaks of "dies palmarum," although without mentioning the procession, in *De Ecclesiasticis Officiis*, I, 28, and *Etymologiae*, VI, 18 (in PL, LXXXIII, 763; LXXXII, 251).

[6] Ed. E. A. Lowe as vol. LVIII of the Henry Bradshaw Society (London, 1920), 558.

[7] Number 2 of the sources.

[8] *Ed. cit.*, n. 3: "ut omnes qui eos *laturi* sunt ita benedictionis" (See the entry 'fero' in any lexicon.).

[9] "In memoriam illius rei nos per ecclesias nostras solemus portare ramos et clamare Hosanna" (In remembrance of this king [Christ] it is fitting that we carry branches through our churches, shouting "hosanna.") (*De officiis*, I, 10, Hanssens, *op. cit.*, II, 58.)

[10] Cf. *Ordo* XXVIII (Andrieu, *op. cit.*, III, 391) *et al.*

[10] Cf. *Ordo* XXVIII (Andrieu, *op. cit.*, III, 391) *et al*; note 8 above; art. "palme" in the *Enciclopedia Cattolica*.

[11] It was not known at Canterbury in Anglo-Saxon times (see number 2 of the sources), neither was it a Norman custom, unless very recent or only local, for there is no mention of the Host in the Palm Sunday procession described by John of Avranches (in number 22 of the sources).

In Lanfranc's version[1] the Host was carried before dawn, quietly and with a minimum of ceremony, outside the city walls to the starting point of the procession which was to take place later. In the procession the Host was carried in the same position as the relics, and when both were carried as was often the case, shared the same pyx.

This form of the procession spread to a number of churches in England and Normandy[2] but it never became general—perhaps due to an unwillingness to adopt such a familiar use of the Blessed Sacrament. In the Germanic regions other forms arose in which a life-size seated figure of Christ was drawn through the streets;[3] but this development belongs properly to the realm of the liturgical drama. The final developments in the procession with the Host seem to have taken place at Sarum, and they have already been discussed.

The Feast of Corpus Christi had at first only a local observance in the diocese of Liège from the year 1246. Soon after in 1264 Urban IV enjoined it upon the whole Church, but for various reasons his decree was not implemented until Clement V renewed it at the council in Vienne in 1311.[4] After this the feast spread rapidly.

Neither in the original institution by Robert, Bishop of Liège, nor in the two following papal decrees was there any mention of a procession with the Blessed Sacrament. The day, in keeping with its rank as a principal feast, would have been celebrated with a procession from the first. But the presence of the Host in the procession seems at the start not to have been general. It is specified in many books, beginning in the thirteenth century. In many others, however, it is not, and the omission of such an important detail, especially where specific directions are given for other processions, must be considered significant.[5]

The practice could easily have been suggested by the Blessed Sacrament in the Palm Sunday procession[6] and may have been taken up first where

[1] Number 20.

[2] Rouen, Coutances, Oxford, York Use, Norwich, St. Mary's (York) (numbers 57, 80, 44, 73, 45, 85).

[3] Such figures may be seen in the museums of Basel, Zürich, Munich, Nürnburg, etc.; for an account of this custom see Young, *op. cit.*, I, 93 ff.

[4] *Catholic Encyclopedia.*

[5] In the Barking ordinal (number 81) where directions are given for the carrying of the feretory on Palm Sunday the directions for Corpus Christi read simply "sicut decet in tali solemnitate" (as would be fitting for such a feast).

[6] At St. Mary's (York) the Host was to be carried "modo quo dictum est in Ramis Palmarum" (number 85).

this was known, but it spread farther. It was known in Cologne in 1279 and in Alberstadt in 1317. In France the Council of Sens of 1320 referred to it. It appears in England at Ipswich in 1325. In Italy it reached Genoa by 1325, Milan by 1336 and Rome by 1350.[1]

THE OTHER PROCESSIONS

The ordinals say very little about these. For the processions after Vespers to the altars and to the crucifix the arrangements followed at Sarum were probably followed generally, since they were made almost entirely with what was at hand for the preceding office. There were candles only, and the thurible which had been used just previously by the celebrant of the day to cense the High Altar during the *Magnificat*. There was no water, cross, or text of the Gospels. The vestments were just as for Vespers except that the celebrant and the choir rulers threw copes over their surplices.

For the counterparts to these processions held in some churches at Matins the arrangements would be similar.

The processions to the altars after Vespers Christmas night and the two nights following were in some places special. On the first night the deacons, on the second the priests, and on the third the boys of the church all carried lighted candles, dressed in silk copes, and played an important part in the commemoration at the altar.

The earliest appearance of these practices seems to be in the eleventh century, in Rouen.[2] Later they can be found in many churches, especially in north-western France and in England, but in a few Benedictine churches elsewhere.[3]

For the blessing of the new fire on Holy Saturday the form at Sarum, with the triple candle, but no cross, and with unlighted tapers and thurible seems to have been general in those churches where the rite involved a procession.

The procession for the consecration of the font at Sarum, which in-

---

[1] E. Dumoutet, *Le Christ selon la chair* (Beauchesne, 1932), 141-142.

[2] Number 22 in the sources.

[3] Amiens, Bayeuz, Châlons, Chartres, Compiègne, Coutances, Rouen; Bury St. Edmund's, Exeter, Hereford, Norwich (and, of course, all the churches of the Sarum Rite); Dijon, Metz, Moggio, Münster (numbers 47, 49, 50, 51, 52, 80, 57, 82, 71, 72, 45, 53, 55, 61, 60). In other places processions on these same occasions may be in no way distinguished (Rome, Rheinau, Barking, numbers 36, 38, 81).

cluded a deacon and sub-deacon, a cross, the oil and chrism, and the candle used in the blessing, is the usual one found in the ordinals.

For the processions of reception most churches used the form of the processions before Mass on great feasts. Sometimes, however, one reads that the cross was omitted.[1]

[1] Cluny, St. Benigne's (Dijon), Bec (see the excerpts from the ordinals printed by Martène, *op. cit.*, IV, 804).

IX. THE SPECIAL CHANTS
1. THE ROGATION ANTIPHONS

The earliest writers to refer to Christian processions make no reference to special chants. We read only of psalms, and of hymns and antiphons "appropriate for the day."[1] For most of the processions there never were special pieces. The length of the list of the Sarum processions with special chants is misleading. Several of these occasions were served with a single hymn; and others made use of antiphons and responds which, although not used otherwise at Sarum, were elsewhere and originally used for different purposes. This was the situation generally throughout the West: there were special chants for only a few of the many solemn processions of the liturgical year. Borrowed pieces served for the rest.

The strict pattern of borrowing by which the Sarum processions were so closely related to the Daily Office was not universal. But a similar use of Office responds, antiphons and versicles and of Mass collects was general. It is difficult to tell the age of this practice. It was a Benedictine custom in centres as far apart as Pontetetto and Tynemouth[2] by about 1100, the time of the earliest processionals, and it is probably a good deal older than this. Borrowed Office antiphons and responds play a part in the processions of the earliest sources.[3]

For the Major Litany, the Rogation Days, in case of too much rain or too little, and when life was threatened through war or other causes, the Sarum books provided special processional antiphons. Including the three pieces* sung during the distribution of the ashes at the beginning of Lent—for they are of the same type and in most other churches were sung in rogation processions—these antiphons number fourteen:

De Ierusalem exeunt
Domine rex deus Abraham
Exaudi domine populum

[1] "Ymnos dicentes vel antiphonas aptas diei ipsi" (Etheria, *ed. cit.*, 537).

[2] Sources 29 and 32.

[3] The Magnificat antiphon *Nativitas tua dei genetrix* in the Compiègne and Senlis graduals (sources 4 and 6); the Office respond *Congregati sunt inimici* in the Old Roman Gradual (source 30).

Exurge domine adiuva
In nomine domini
Inundaverunt aque
Libera domine populum
Non nos demergat
Numquid est in idolis
Respice domine
Surgite sancti
*Exaudi nos domine quoniam
*Immutemur habitu
*Iuxta vestibulum.

This is roughly consistent with the number of special antiphons provided for the same purposes in books of other churches in the later medieval period. This fourteen, however, is only a remnant of a much larger and widespread repertory which in an increasingly secular world had fallen mostly into disuse.

The oldest service books devote a good deal of space to rogation processions. The ninth-century gradual from Senlis, and the Corbie Gradual, written about the year 900,[1] each contain nearly a hundred rogation antiphons. Altogether, the earliest Gregorian sources, graduals and tropers written from about the years 800 to 1100, contain about one hundred and fifty. The list which follows contains, in fact, one hundred and fifty-four antiphons. But to say exactly how many there were is impossible. Some of this number may be Office antiphons—untraceable because they happen not to be current in any of the few surviving sources of this early period. Almost certainly a number of pieces have been completely lost; the decay of the repertory occurred early, and part of it doubtless became obsolete before the date of the oldest surviving service books.

The following alphabetical list shows the distribution of the special rogation antiphons in the oldest French, Aquitanian, German and Italian manuscripts, and the concordances in the Visigothic, Milanese and Old Roman books.

At least two ancient sources for processional pieces have been lost in fairly recent times. Pamelius used three manuscripts, uncertainly identified but evidently very old, for his text edition of the Gradual published in his *Liturgicon* of 1571.[2] It is believed that his main source was the Mont-Blandin manuscript,[3] but this contains very few of the

[1] Sources 6 and 7.
[2] Reprinted in *Patrologia Latina*, LXXVIII, col. 682 ff.
[3] Source 3. See Hesbert, *op. cit.*, XV.

forty or so processional antiphons included in the 1571 edition. It can be supposed that the unknown source (or sources) for these chants is not one of those at hand, for included for the *Liturgicon* processions are pieces not found elsewhere, and certain unique variants: "Placet Jerusalem civitas" for *Jerusalem civitas*, "Desclamemus omnes" for *Exclamemus omnes*, etc. The second case is that of the Laon Gradual,[1] which lost most of its rogation antiphons in the eighteenth century when the folios which contained the pieces for the Rogation Days were detached to be carried in the processions.[2]

The antiphons of the Limoges troper, Paris, B. N. lat. 1240,[3] are represented mostly by cues, and sometimes not enough is given to make identification certain.

Table 1

The distribution of the rogation antiphons in twenty of the oldest chant sources

	Mont-Blandin (3) (VIII-IX)	Compiègne (4) (IX)	Senlis (6) (IX)	Corbie (7) (IX-X)	Laon (8) (IX-X)	Chartres (10) (X)	Mont-Rénaud (12) (X)	Limoges (11) (X)	Limoges (16) (X-XI)	Limoges (17) (X-XI)	St. Yrieix (23) (XI)	Mainz (13) (X)	St. Gall (15) (X)	Einsiedeln (19) (X-XI)	Nonantola (26) (XI)	Novalesa (27) (XI)	Benevento (28) (XI-XII)	Milan (35)	León (1)
Ambulabunt sancti tui[4]															x				
Ambulate sancti dei… ad locum		x	x			x		x	x	x	x		x	x	x				
Ambulate sancti dei… ingredimini		x	x			x		x	x	x	x		x	x	x				
Anima in angustia		x	x																
Annuntiate inter gentes		x	x			x	x	x	x	x	x		x	x					
Archangelus domini							x												
Aridaverunt montes															x				
Auribus percipe		x	x																
Benedic domine domum						x		x	x	x			x		x				
Benedicat dominus sacerdos												x							
Benedicat vos deus						x													

[1] Source 8.

[2] See the note on the flyleaf of the manuscript and the Introduction to volume X of *Paléographie Musicale*.

[3] Source 11.

[4] This antiphon, as "Ibunt sancti" is also found in the *Liturgicon* (1571) of Pamelius.

Table 1—*Continued*

	Mont-Blandin (3) (VIII-IX)	Compiègne (4) (IX)	Senlis (6) (IX)	Corbie (7) (IX-X)	Laon (8) (IX-X)	Chartres (10) (X)	Mont-Rénaud (12) (X)	Limoges (11) (X)	Limoges (16) (X-XI)	Limoges (17) (X-XI)	St. Yrieix (23) (XI)	Mainz (13) (X)	St. Gall (15) (X)	Einsiedeln (19) (X-XI)	Nonantola (26) (XI)	Novalesa (27) (XI)	Benevento (28) (XI-XII)	Milan (35)	León (1)	Rome (30)
edicat vos spiritus[1]													x							
edicat vos... maiestas[1]						x			x			x	x							
edictus dominus		x	x																	
iste qui regnas[2]															x					
nentissime exaudi				x		x			x	x				x	x					
gnovimus domine impietates... t iniquitates		x	x																	
gnovimus domine impietates... uia		x	x																	x
gnovimus domine quia												x	x							
afitemini domino filii	x	x	x			x	x	x	x	x	x			x	x	x	x			x
averte nos		x	x																	
avertere domine		x	x			x		x	x	x	x			x	x	x				x
avertimini omnes						x							x			x				
n iocunditate		x	x	x		x	x	x	x	x	x	x	x	x	x				x	x
stodi domine gregem							x	x	x											
stodit dominus animas		x	x			x	x	x	x	x				x	x					x
Jerusalem exeunt		x	x			x	x	x	x	x	x			x	x	x			x	x
precamur te domine		x	x			x	x	x	x	x	x			x	x	x	x	x		x
te in te refugium																x				
tribulatione clamamus															x		x	x		
us benedicat qui[1]													x							
us canticum novum		x	x																	
us de celis																x				
us deus noster respice															x					
us in adiutorium		x	x																	
us qui es benedictus								x	x	x				x						
cit dominus videte		x	x																	

[1] *Benedicat vos ... maiestas* is a long antiphon with sections beginning "Benedicat vos spiritus," and "Ille vos benedicat qui de celis." The two antiphons *Benedicat vos spiritus* and *Deus benedicat qui* which follow *Benedicat vos ... maiestas* in the Mainz Troper are probably no more than separated sections.

[2] This antiphon had some currency, for it is included by Pamelius.

Table 1 —*Continued*

	Mont-Blandin (3) (VIII-IX)	Compiègne (4) (IX)	Senlis (6) (IX)	Corbie (7) (IX-X)	Laon (8) (IX-X)	Chartres (10) (X)	Mont-Rénaud (12) (X)	Limoges (11) (X)	Limoges (16) (X-XI)	Limoges (17) (X-XI)	St. Yrieix (23) (XI)	Mainz (13) (X)	St. Gall (15) (X)	Einsiedeln (19) (X-XI)	Nonantola (26) (XI)	Novalesa (27) (XI)	Benevento (28) (XI-XII)	Milan (35)	León (1)
Dimitte domine peccata nostra		x	x			x	(x)					x	x						
Dimitte domine peccata populi		x	x			x	x	(x)	x	x		x	x	x					
Dimitte nobis domine						x		x	x	x	x	x	x	x	x		x		
Domine defecimus		x	x																
Domine deus noster Abraham		x	x																
Domine deus noster qui	x	x	x			x	x	x	x	x	x	x	x	x	x	x			
Domine deus omnipotens[1]												x							
Domine imminuti sumus		x	x			x	x	x	x	x	x	x	x	x	x		x		
Domine miserere nostri		x	x			x		x	x	x	x		x	x	x				
Domine ne taceas		x	x																
Domine non est alius		x	x			x	x	x	x	x	x		x	x	x				
Domine non irascatur		x	x																
Domine omnipotens		x	x																
Domine rex deus Abraham		x	x	x		x	x	x	x	x	x		x	x	x				
Domine rex omnipotens																	x		
Domine rigans montes		x	x			x		x	x	x	x		x	x	x				
Domine si iratus fueris								x	x	x						x		x	
Ecce populus custodiens		x	x	x		x	x	x	x	x	x		x	x	x				
Ecce sion filii		x	x																
Ego sum deus patrum	x	x	x	x		x	x	x	x	x	x	x	x	x	x	x	x		
Exaudi deus deprecationem		x	x			x		x	x	x	x		x	x	x				
Exaudi domine deprecationem servorum						x	x	(x)		x	x		x	x	x				
Exaudi domine lacrimas		x	x				(x)						x						
Exaudi domine populum... confitentem		x	x	x		x	x	(x)	x	x			x	x	x		x		
Exaudi domine populum ... toto																	x		
Exaudi nos deus in veritate		x	x																
Exaudi nos domine qui		x	x	x		x	x	x	x	x	x		x	x	x		x		
Exaudi nos domine quoniam	x	x	x	x	x	x	x	x	x	x	x	x	x	x		x	x		

[1] This piece can be found in at least one later source, the processional Ms 222 of Rouen (source 57).

Table 1 —*Continued*

	Mont-Blandin (3) (VIII-IX)	Compiègne (4) (IX)	Senlis (6) (IX)	Corbie (7) (IX-X)	Laon (8) (IX-X)	Chartres (10) (X)	Mont-Rénaud (12) (X)	Limoges (11) (X)	Limoges (16) (X-XI)	Limoges (17) (X-XI)	St. Yrieix (23) (XI)	Mainz (13) (X)	St. Gall (15) (X)	Einsiedeln (19) (X-XI)	Nonantola (26) (XI)	Novalesa (27) (XI)	Benevento (28) (XI-XII)	Milan (35)	León (1)	Rome (30)
lamemus omnes	x	x	x	x		x	x	x	x	x	x	x	x	x	x	x	x			x
e sancti orate¹											x									
rge domine adiuva																				
rge libera nos															x					
domine vindictam		x	x																	
sti magnalia		x	x																	
dete iusti		x	x																	
gem tuum domine														x		x				
niliamini sub potenti		x	x																	
nutemur habitu	x	x	x	x	x	x	x	x	x	x	x	x	x	x		x	x			
ivitate domine															x	x				
ina domine ... et audi		x	x			x	(x)	x	x	x		x	x	x				x		
ina domine ... et exaudi²		x	x				(x)													
edere benedicite		x	x					x	x	x		x	x							
uitates nostre	x	x	x			x	x	x	x	x	x	x	x	x	x	x	x	x		x
liniven civitatum							x											x		
omine domini³							x											x		
anctis gloriosus		x				x		x	x	x	x	x	x							
ribulationibus																x				
daverunt aque		x	x	x		x	x	x	x	x	x	x	x	x		x				x
cantes dominum		x	x			x	x	x	x	x	x	x	x	x	x	x				
cavimus et vidimus		x	x																	
itia tua sicut montes		x	x																	
a vestibulum et altare	x	x	x	x	x	x	x	x	x	x	x	x	x	x		x	x			
salem civitas sancta		x	x					x	x	x						x	x			
ra domine populum		x	x	x		x	x	x	x	x	x	x	x	x			x			
ra nos domine		x	x																	
ia vita in morte																	x		x	

¹ This antiphon had some currency, for it is included in a processional from Toulouse (source 34).

² This is a very short piece, and perhaps an Office antiphon. The Worcester Antiphoner (source 46) contains a piece whose text differs only at the close.

³ This antiphon was widespread later; it is found at Tynemouth (source 32), at Worcester (source 46), and of course at Sarum.

Table 1 —*Continued*

	Mont-Blandin (3) (VIII-IX)	Compiègne (4) (IX)	Senlis (6) (IX)	Corbie (7) (IX-X)	Laon (8) (IX-X)	Chartres (10) (X)	Mont-Rénaud (12) (X)	Limoges (11) (X)	Limoges (16) (X-XI)	Limoges (17) (X-XI)	St. Yrieix (23) (XI)	Mainz (13) (X)	St. Gall (15) (X)	Einsiedeln (19) (X-XI)	Nonantola (26) (XI)	Novalesa (27) (XI)	Benevento (28) (XI-XII)	Milan (35)	León (1)
Memento congregationis		x	x																
Miserere domine et dic		x	x					(x)		x				x					
Miserere domine plebi		x	x	x		x	x	(x)	x	x			x	x	x		x		
Miserere nobis domine	x																	x	
Miserere nostri deus		x	x																
Misericors es domine		x	x																
Monasterium istud¹												x	(x)	x					
Multa sunt domine		x	x	x		x	x	x	x	x			x	x	x		x		
Nec observavimus																	x		
Ne nos demergat tempestas		x																	
Non in iustificationibus						x		x	x	x	x		x	x	x		x		
Non nos demergat domine		x	x			x		x	x	x	x		x	x	x		x		
Nos peccavimus domine															x				
Numquid est in idolis		x	x			x	x	x	x	x			x	x	x				x
Numquid valet manus		x	x																x
Omnipotens deus mestorum												x	x	x			x		
Omnipotens deus supplices						x					x			x	x				
Oportet nos mundum						x		x	x	x			x	x	x		x		
Oremus dilectissimi						x	x	x	x	x	x		x	x	x	x	x		
Parce domine parce	x					x	x	x	x	x	x	x	x	x	x	x	x		
Pax huic domui											x		x	x					
Peccavimus domine et tu		x	x			x	x	(x)	x	x			x	x	x		x		
Peccavimus domine in iuste²		x	x					(x)											
Peccavimus domine peccavimus tibi						x	x	(x)	x	x					x		x		
Peccavimus tibi deus																x			
Per memetipsum		x	x																
Platee Jerusalem						x		x	x	x			x	x	x				
Populus Sion convertimini	x	x	x			x	x	x	x	x			x	x	x		x		x
Posuisti domine		x	x																
Pro pace regum																x	x		
Propitius esto domine						x		x	x	x	x					x			

¹ This occurs, not set apart in any way, as the last section of the antiphon *Signum salutis* in the St. Gall Gradual (source 15). See note 3, p. 127.

² This is found later in Paris, Bibl. Nat. lat. 10511, f. 253v.

Table 1 — *Continued*

	Mont-Blandin (3) (VIII-IX)	Compiègne (4) (IX)	Senlis (6) (IX)	Corbie (7) (IX-X)	Laon (8) (IX-X)	Chartres (10) (X)	Mont-Rénaud (12) (X)	Limoges (11) (X)	Limoges (16) (X-XI)	Limoges (17) (X-XI)	St. Yrieix (23) (XI)	Mainz (13) (X)	St. Gall (15) (X)	Einsiedeln (19) (X-XI)	Nonantola (26) (XI)	Novalesa (27) (XI)	Benevento (28) (XI-XII)	Milan (35)	León (1)	Rome (30)
opter peccata nostra															x			x		
i cognoscis omnia												x								
i siccasti mare															x					
cordare mei domine		x	x														x			x
dime domine de interitu	x	x															x			x
spice cuncta																	x			
spice domine quia		x	x			x		x	x	x	x		x	x	x					x
spice domine quomodo		x	x																	
gamus te[1]															x			x		
pti sunt fontes															x					
lvum fac populum[2]	x																			
nctificabo te			x																	
nctos portamus						x									x					
nctus deus sanctus								x	x	x	x					x				
clauso celo pluvia												x			x					
cut exaudisti domine												x			x					
cut pastor portat ovem									x			x					x			
fecissemus		x	x									x					x			
num salutis pone[3]												x		x	(x)	x	x		x	
nosmetipsos		x	x																	
t occuli tui															x					
dominus deus noster		x	x					x	x	x										
b altare domine[4]															x					x
per populum tuum												x	x	x						
gite sancti						x						x	x							
rribile est Christe[5]																	x	x		
mor et tremor						x	x				x	x			x		x			
a est domine		x	x																	
i sunt misericordie		x	x			x						x					x			
quequo domine adhuc		x	x																	

[1] This chant is called a respond in the Nonantola Troper; it is discussed later.

[2] This is included by Pamelius.

[3] In the Einsiedeln Gradual (source 19) *Signum salutis* appears as a verse of *Monasterium istud.* See note 1, p. 126.   [4] This piece is very like an Office antiphon.

[5] In the Nonantola Troper (source 26) this appears as the last part of the antiphon *Nos peccavimus domine.*

On the basis of the texts, the rogation antiphons fall naturally into three or four groups. The majority are prayers and of a general nature, seeking God's mercy for sin, or help in some unspecified difficulty:

Parce Domine, parce populo tuo quem redemisti Christe sanguine tuo ut non in eternum irascaris nobis

Spare, Lord, spare your people whom you redeemed through your blood, the blood of Christ, and damn us not through all eternity.

Dimitte Domine peccata populi tui secundum multitudinem misericordie tue, sicut propitius fuisti patribus nostris, propitius esto et nobis.

Forgive, Lord, the sins of your people according to the bounty of your mercy; as you were helpful unto our fathers be even so unto us.

Omnipotens Deus, mestorum consolatio laborantium fortitudo, perveniant ad te preces de quacumque tribulatione clamantium, ut omnes sibi in necessitatibus suis misericordiam tuam gaudeant adfuisse.

Omnipotent God, consolation of the sorrowful, strength of them that labour, let the prayers of those who plead for whatever tribulation reach you that all, being given what is necessary each for his need, may praise your mercy.

Exaudi nos, Domine, qui exaudisti Ionam de ventre ceti; exaudi nos clamantes, qui exaudisti David prostratum et iacentem in cilicio, clamantes et dicentes: Parce, defende plasma tuum, Deus noster.

Hear us, Lord, who heard Jonah in the belly of the whale; hear our cries who heeded David prostrate and cast down in the dust, hear[our cries] as we sing: Spare us, our God, protect those made in your image.

A number of antiphons are prayers embodying more specific requests:

For rain.

Aridaverunt montes, siccaverunt flumina, terra fructum negavit; dona nobis pluviam: non peccavit terra nec radices montium, sed nos peccavimus; parce nobis, Domine, dona nobis pluviam.

The mountains are scorched, the rivers have dried up, the earth withholds its fruits; give us rain: it is not the land which has sinned, nor the mountain valleys; it is we who have sinned; spare us, Lord, grant us rain.

Others of this type are:

Domine Rex Deus Abraham
Domine Rex omnipotens
Domine rigans montes
Exaudi Domine lacrimas
Exaudi Domine populum tuum confitentem
Exaudi Domine populum tuum toto
Numquid est in idolis
Recordare Domine
Respice cuncta quia
Respice Domine quia
Si clauso celo.

For the end of rain.

Inundaverunt aque, Domine, super capita nostra; invocavimus nomen tuum de lacu novissimo ne avertas faciem tuam a singultu nostro.

Lord, the waters have burst over our heads; we invoke your name for [relief from] these unheard-of waters; turn not your face from our tears.

Other antiphons with similar texts are:

Deus canticum novum
Exaudi nos Deus in veritate
Non nos demergat
Pro pace regum
Qui siccasti mare
Per memetipsum
Rupti sunt fontes.

For deliverance from war or other physical danger.

Libera, Domine, populum tuum de manu mortis, et plebem istam protegat dextera tua, ut viventes benedicamus te Domine Deus noster.

Deliver, Lord, from the hand of death your people; with your right hand protect them, that living they might bless you, the Lord our God.

Others of this type are:

Benedictus Dominus qui
Deus deus noster respice
Domine Deus noster Abraham
Domine miserere nostri
Exurge libera nos
Fac Domine vindictam
Miserere Domine et dic
Miserere nostri Deus omnium
Respice Domine quomodo
Tua est Domine.

For the protection of the convent.

Signum salutis pone Domine in domibus istis, et non permittas introire angelum percutientem in domibus in quibus habitamus; de celo pone signum tuum, Domine, et protege nos et non erit in nobis plaga nocens.

Place the mark of safety, Lord, upon these houses, and permit not the Destroying Angel to enter into those in which we live; from heaven make your mark, Lord, and keep from us the crippling blow.

Similar are:

Benedic Domine domum
Deus de celis
Invocantes Dominum
Monasterium istud
Pax huic domui
Sint occuli tui.

Processions for other specific emergencies, for example "against pestilence," are sometimes found. Appropriate versicles and collects are provided for these services, but the antiphons are drawn from the already-mentioned classifications.

A number of pieces are not prayers at all. Some, intended to give comfort, use language reminiscent of the Prophets:

Confitemini Domino, filii Israel, quia non est alius deus preter eum; ipsi liberavit nos propter misericordiam suam; aspicite que fecit nobiscum, et enarremus omnia mirabilia eius.

We trust in the Lord, Sons of Israel, for there is no other god but he; in his mercy he has set us free; take heed of what he has done for us, and proclaim his many wonders.

Others of this type are:

Ego sum Deus
Convertimini ad Deum
Cum venerit Filius
Ecce populus custodiens
Sicut pastor portat.

Some others have texts of a more or less joyful nature:

Platee Ierusalem gaudebunt et omnes vici eius canticum letitie dicant.

Jerusalem's pavements rejoice, and all her streets sing the canticle of joy.

Cum iocunditate exibitis et cum gaudio deducimini nam et montes et colles exilient expectantes vos cum gaudio.

Go forth in joy, and with rejoicing lead the way, for the hills and mountains themselves rejoice, and await you in gladness.

Sanctos portamus sanctorum laudes dicimus et nos in terra psalimus in celis canunt angeli: pax in celo, pax in terra, pax in omni populo, pax in sacerdotibus et in omnibus sanctis eius.

We bear the saints, and sing their praises; we sing on earth, the angels sing in heaven: Peace on high, peace on earth, peace to all people, peace to his priests and all his saints.

Of the same kind are:

Ambulabunt sancti tui
Ambulate sancti dei ad locum
Ambulate sancti dei ingredimini
Annuntiate inter gentes
Custodit Dominus animas
De Ierusalem exeunt
Ecce populus custodiens
Ecce Sion filii
Exite sancti orate
Gaudete iusti
Ierusalem civitas
In civitate Domine
Ingredere benedicte
In nomine Domini
Surgite sancti.

The explanation is that these pieces were in honour of the relics of the saints which were carried in the rogation processions. This is made clear by the texts, as in *Sanctos portamus*, and in the earliest Gregorian service books, where these antiphons are found under the rubric "ad reliquias deducendas" or directions to this effect.[1] These chants were sung, and were perhaps originally intended for the ceremony of the dedication of churches, which involved the solemn transfer of relics to the new altar. Some of the antiphons figure in the oldest dedication rites. In the Gradual of León,[2] under the general heading "de sacratione basilice" and the rubric "antiphone de processione reliquiarum,"[3] can be found *Dum iocunditate*, *In nomine domini*, and *De Jerusalem*.[4] The melodies, however, are similar in style to the penitential antiphons; and already in the earliest manuscripts, relics pieces are prescribed for the rogation processions. *Cum iocunditate*, however inappropriate it may seem, can even be found as an antiphon "de quacumque tribulatione."

These joyful relics pieces were also sung for festive processions of the saints ("de nataliciis sanctorum"), and perhaps for processions on

[1] Sources 4, 6, etc.

[2] Source 1.

[3] Folio 264 ff.

[4] A number of the *Ordines Romani* (*ed. cit.*) mention these relics pieces in a similar context.

ordinary Sundays, assuming that "crucem" in the rubric "ad crucem deducendam" refers to the usual processional cross.[1]

All the antiphons have prose texts, and with two or three exceptions they are free compositions. *Salvum fac populum* uses Psalm XXVII, 9, but this fact and its brevity may indicate that it is originally an Office antiphon. *Exurge Domine adiuva*, with one slight variation, is Psalm XLIII, 26. It too is very short. *Dimitte nobis Domine*, but for a word, is the conclusion of the Lord's Prayer, and of course also scriptural. Although the texts are not usually drawn verbatim from the Bible, some borrow from it extensively; indeed, biblical phraseology, ranging from Genesis to the Apocalypse, is one of their most conspicuous features. Compare the following antiphon incipits and scriptural passages.

Per memetipsum iuravi, dicit Dominus, non audiciam ultra aquas diluvi ...	Per memetipsum iuravi, dicit Dominus, quia fecisti ... (Genesis, XXII, 16)
Inclina, Domine, aurem tuam et audi respice de celo et vide afflictionem...	Inclina aurem tuam, et audi; aperi, Domine, occulos ... (IV Kings, XIX, 16)
Domine rigans montes de superioribus tuis de fructu operum tuorum Domine saciabitur terra quam magnificata sunt opera tua...	Rigans montes de superioribus suis; de fructu operum tuorum satiabitur terra; prodecens foenum iumentis, (Psalm CIII, 13)
In nomine Domini Dei nostri ambulabimus nos, et omnes populi; quoniam in Sion ...	Nos autem ambulabimus in nomine Domini Dei nostri (Micah, IV, 5)
Ego sum Deus patrum vestrorum dicit Dominus; videns vidi afflictionem populi mei, et gemitum eius audivi, et descendi liberare eos.	Ego sum Deus patrum tuorum, Deus Abraham ... Videns vidi afflictionem populi mei qui est in Aegypto ... et descendi liberare eos. (Acts, VII, 32-34)

The texts exhibit little variety and, except for the biblical figures, have no particular literary merit. Those which are prayers share certain of the features of the collects. Among the scriptural catch-phrases are the ubiquitous cliches: "oremus dilectissimi," "propter nomen tuam," "propter misericordiam tuam," "parce, Domine," "Domine Deus noster," "Domine Deus Israel," "omnipotens Deus," "Exurge, Domine," "Dimitte, Domine," "Exaudi, Deus." There is a kind of mechanical prolixity and, frequently in the longer pieces, extended parallelism:

[1] See sources 3 through 8.

(from *Timor et tremor*)
  Sed tu, Deus omnipotens, misericors et miserator, misertus es miseris...

(from *Omnipotens Deus supplices*)
  per intercessionem novem ordinum angelorum, throni, et dominationes, et principatus, et potestates, cherubim quoque et seraphim...

(from *Oportet nos*)
  te laudamus, Domine, omnipotens qui sedes super cherubim et seraphim exaudi nos; te laudant angeli et archangeli; te venerant prophete et apostoli, te adoramus, te veneramus ...

(from *Christe qui regnas*)
  Christe qui regnas in celis et sedes ad dexteram patris, et habitas inter angelos et archangelos, thronos et dominationes, et apostoli tui te laudant, et martyres tibi hymnum cantant; confessores in paradiso concordant...

One curious feature worth noting is that Christ is mentioned in only a handful of the antiphons. But an Old Testament flavour is perhaps to be expected in view of the obvious parallel between the medievals in procession and the People of Israel in the desert.

THE MELODIES

About a hundred of the rogation antiphons, approximately two-thirds of the Gregorian repertory, survive in notations which can be read accurately for pitch. The music for a few others exists in outline in cheironomic neumes. The basis of the following account consists mainly of transcriptions made from the St. Yrieix Gradual, a manuscript of the eleventh century.[1] The pieces not found in this book have been studied from their earliest diastematic source. As a rule, the earliest books are the most desirable for the study of the Chant; for one reason, because they often preserve nuances not transmitted by later manuscripts. Nevertheless, there was reason for choosing as a main source for chants not sung at Sarum the St. Yrieix manuscript over the Limoges Troper, Paris, B.N. lat. 1121, which is a little earlier. The Aquitainian neumes of the earlier book, written *in campo aperto*, indicate the intervals correctly but leave the tonality of the chants in doubt. The St. Yrieix book employs much the same Aquitainian notation, but one neume, a *pes* with a semi-circular *virga* is used consistently to indicate the scale half-step. This same *pes* appears in the Limoges Troper, but it can be shown that in this book the neume has no consistent tonal implications. With the help

[1] Source 23.

of the St. Yrieix Gradual and other later books it would of course have been possible to determine the tonality and make accurate transcriptions of a good many of the pieces from the Limoges Troper. But it was thought best to take as many pieces as possible from one source, in order that regional variations in the antiphons should not obscure melodic relationships.

The Tonality

Precise transcriptions can be made of one hundred and two of the rogation antiphons. Five of this number are available only in Ambrosian or Old Roman versions and have been excluded from this account. This is not to suggest that the Old Roman tradition has nothing to do with the Gregorian. But in the matter of tonality the Old Roman books so frequently disagree with the consensus of Gregorian sources that it seemed better not to count these few pieces. Ten additional antiphons are found in notations which do not indicate the position of the scale half-step. These have been assigned to modes, in most cases without misgivings, on the basis of melodic figures which are generally recognized to have tonal or scale-step implications in Gregorian Chant — chiefly an intonation figure of the D mode:

Ex. 37.

and the melodic ascending triads on the notes C and F. The modal attribution is confirmed for most of these pieces by the appearance of the *quilisma* and a special *torculus*, neumes whose operation in the St. Yrieix Gradual, at least for the rogation pieces, seems confined to certain scale degrees: E and B for the first neume, and C for the second. This ten brings the total of the melodies available for study to one hundred and seven.

There is a problem encountered in assigning some of the antiphons which close with the Alleluia. This (to us) inappropriate conclusion for penitential chants was evidently thought necessary to conform to the practice for all other antiphons sung in the Easter Season: the Rogation Days and the Feast of St. Mark—the fixed occasions of the rogation processions—both fall before Ascension. A few pieces, of a joyful character in honour of relics carried in the rogation processions, end in a way to leave no doubt about the authenticity of the conclusion. The final words of *Custodi Domine gregem*, for example, are "ut gaudentes dicant: Alleluia." But the evidence of the earliest sources, where these Alleluias are not present, and the diversity in practice indicate that these appendages, except in a few cases, formed no part of the original chants.

The difficulty is this: in several instances the final of the antiphon proper and the final of the Alleluia are different. A number of the antiphons appear to have been adjusted, in the manner of the psalm-tone *differentiae*, to lead smoothly, without cadence, into the initial figure of the Alleluia. *Timor et tremor* is a particularly interesting example, for both versions survive. In the St. Yrieix Gradual it concludes as follows:

Ex. 38. Source 23, folio 138.

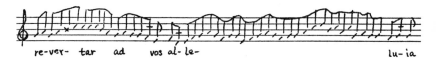

In the Nonantola Troper[1] the antiphon closes on G:

Ex. 39. Source 26, folio 167.

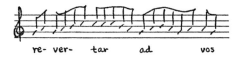

In all such cases the chants have been assigned according to the last note of the Alleluia.

These are the figures resulting from the classification of the pieces according to their *finalis*—first, those which are not in doubt: D, thirty-seven pieces; E, seventeen; F, nine; G, twenty-nine. Three antiphons close on A; two on C. Including the ten pieces whose tonality is not as certain the figures read: D, forty-one; E, nineteen; F, nine; G, thirty-three. The manuscripts which would be of use have been compared on the question of tonality. No attempt has been made to record all the discrepancies, but it is interesting to note that the Italian books seem to favour higher readings, although not, as a rule, agreeing themselves.

[1] Source 26.

In a dozen or so cases in the Nonantola Troper, and in the Beneventan and Old Roman graduals,[1] antiphons which in other manuscripts of the list and in later sources are usually written in the D mode appear a fourth or a fifth higher on G or A; similarly F pieces are found a fifth higher, and G pieces up a fourth.

A classification which takes account of melodic characteristics, although less certain than one based on the finals alone, will more accurately show the distribution of the rogation antiphons with respect to the standard Gregorian system of four *maneriae*. The antiphons ending on A seem to belong to the protus tonality. For two of them it may be a case of transposition. *Sint occuli tui* opens with a characteristic D mode figure a fifth higher:

Ex. 40. Source 26, folio 186v.

Sint oc-cu-li tui a-perti

The other, *Multa sunt Domine*, can be found as a D piece in later sources.[2] The third, *Deprecamur te*, opens with the characteristic protus formula untransposed:

Ex. 41. Source 23, folio 135.

De-pre ca- mur te

and this suggests that the concluding A is to be thought of as a *co-finalis* of the D mode. Similarly, two of the pieces, *Miserere Domine et dic*, and *Recordare Domine*, which usually close on F, properly belong to the D group. In the Nonantola Troper the first of these does, in fact, cadence on D (folio 178v).

Making these adjustments, one hundred and five antiphons divide into the four *maneriae* as follows: forty-six are protus, nineteen deuterus, seven tritus, and thirty-three tetrardus. Counting as plagal those antiphons

[1] Sources 26, 25, 30.
[2] Rouen processional, source 57, folio 49v.

whose melodies descend to the fourth below the final,[1] they divide into modes as follows: protus: thirty authentic and sixteen plagal; deuterus: all nineteen authentic; tritus: three authentic, four plagal; tetrardus: twenty-one authentic, twelve plagal. (These figures may be understood roughly as percentages.)

Range

The range of the antiphons is from a sixth to an eleventh. About three quarters of the pieces use an octave or less, more than half, an octave or a seventh. In nearly every case this range lies within the usual Gregorian ambitus for the mode as given in the tenth-century *Dialogus de Musica*:[2] mode 1, a ninth, c′ to d″; mode 2, a tenth, g to b′; mode 3, a ninth, d′ to e″; mode 5 (mode 4 is not represented in the rogation antiphons), a ninth, e′ to f″; mode 6, a ninth, c′ to d″; mode 7, a tenth, f′ to a″; mode 8, a tenth, c′ to e″. A few pieces do exceed this ambitus, but only by a note or two: some of the third mode pieces descend to c′; one second mode antiphon, *Sicut pastor portat*, touches the low f. Only three of the second mode pieces contain the low g.

Length

For the sake of convenience in comparing them to the chants of the Mass and Office, the length of the rogation antiphons has been estimated roughly in lines as the pieces would appear printed in the format of the Solesmes *Liber Usualis*, *Graduale*, or *Antiphonale*. The pieces range from one to over eighteen lines long; but almost half are between four and six lines, and more than three quarters between three and seven.

Melodic Characteristics

The antiphons employ from one to twelve or more notes per syllable. In any one chant, groups of two and three notes predominate, but longer groups occur almost as frequently, melismas of nine and ten notes being

---

[1] Cf. *Quomodo de Arithmetica Procedit Musica*, Gerbert, *Scriptores*, II, 55 ff. According to this treatise one of the pieces, *Ambulate sancti ... ingredimini*, should be considered plagal since its range, although not including the lower fourth below the final, does not reach to the upper fifth. But the companion piece, *Ambulate sancti ... ad locum*, whose melody begins identically, has the required range for assignment to the authentic mode, and the two certainly belong together.

[2] Gerbert, *Scriptores*, I, 251.

quite common. The distribution of these groups is not even; the longer ones occur mainly on the last and on the accented syllables of words. Interspersed are single notes, most often between groups; but in a large majority of the antiphons series or three of four single notes do occur, and syllabic passages of nine and ten notes appear occasionally.

Most of the melodic progressions are stepwise. Leaps are rarer as they are larger; only three examples occur of the sixth. Successive thirds, up and down, are frequent. Thirds-plus-fourths and thirds-plus-fifths do not occur. Fourths-plus-thirds are found, both ascending and descending. The fourth-plus-fourth is not found, except in the Alleluias. Fifths-plus-thirds appear rarely, only ascending:

Ex. 42. From *Respice domine quia*, Ms Rawl. lit. d. 4, folio 97v.

There are no combinations of fifths and fourths, nor of larger intervals.

Many of the antiphons, more than a third, contain conspicuous reminiscences of psalm-tones, or short passages of recitation on one pitch:

Ex. 43. Source 33, folio 253v.

Source 23, folio 140.

Ms Rawl. it. d. 4, folio 96v.

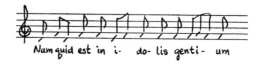

Strophici of two and three notes can be found in practically every anti-phon:

Ex. 44. Ms Rawl. lit. d. 4., folio 98v.

Scale passages of five, or in one instance of six notes occur in more than a quarter of the pieces:

Ex. 45. *Exaudi domine lacrimas,* Source 23, folio 139.

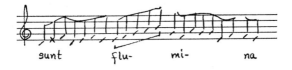

Ex. 46. *Ambulate sancti ... ingredimini,* Source 23, folio 137v.

Ex. 47. *Exite sancti,* Source 23, folio 137v.

Internal repetition is an important feature of the melodies of the rogation antiphons. The most frequent sort, found in more than a third of the pieces, involves the recurrence of a motive, sometimes only very bief, at the start of successive phrases of the text:

Ex. 48. Source 23, folio 133v.

Some of these head-motives are much longer:

Ex. 49. Source 23, folio 139v.

Ex. 50. Ms Rawl. lit. d. 4, folio 98.

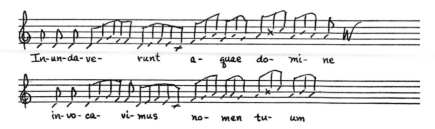

In view of this characteristic it is not surprising that in certain manuscripts antiphons have combined into larger units, or sections have become separated to lead an independent existence. Three antiphons are made of *Benedicat vos... maiestatem* in the Mainz Troper.[1] The latter part of *Nos peccavimus Domine* is found separated as the antiphon *Terribile est Christe* in

---

[1] Source 13, folio 48v.

a Beneventan source.[1] Other examples of this have been noted in the alphabetical list of the pieces.

In some cases a cadence will be repeated for successive text phrases:

Ex. 51. *Non nos demergat*, Ms Rawl. lit. d. 4, folio 98v.

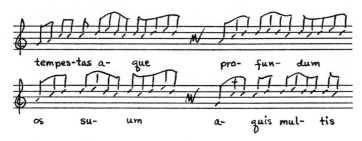

Other kinds of internal repetition are also to be found, with and without textual correspondence:

Ex. 52. *Populus Sion*, Source 23, folio 134.

Ex. 53. *In sanctis gloriosus*, Source 23, folio 137v.

Ex. 54. *Sanctos portamus*, Source 26, folio 181.

[2] Source 28, folio 161.

Ex. 55. *Libera domine populum*, Source 23, folio 139v.

de ma-   nu mor-   tis   ut vi-ven- tes be- ne-di-ca- mus

Altogether, the internal repetition of segments of melody—not merely brief standard motives—is a feature in about a third of the antiphons.

None of these characteristics of the rogation antiphons is un-Gregorian. One or two of the findings of Apel's study would suggest otherwise, and these must be challenged here. He speaks of the "almost complete absence of ... the upward fourth-plus-third" as a melodic progression in Gregorian Chant and writes that he was able to find only three examples, all from Offertory verses.[1] This progression, which occurs frequently in the rogation pieces, is not rare elsewhere. It is so common in the antiphons of the Office as to be a feature of Gevaert's *theme 6*,[2] and examples in the Mass pieces, in Introits, Graduals, Offertories, Alleluias, and Communions can be found with little trouble. Apel also concludes that internal repetitions, although characteristic of Gregorian chant, are "on the whole, exceptional."[3] Such repetition is found in about a quarter of the rogation antiphons, but it is just as frequently found, for example, in the Offertories, and must be considered a feature of the ornate chants.

Melodic Relationships between the Antiphons

To begin with, there are a few short intonation figures common to a number of rogation antiphons. In the first mode (protus authenticus) there are two recurring formulas, the first, which has already been encountered, featuring the notes d' a' b' a', the second, d' c' f' a':

Ex. 56.

Both of these occur equally at the beginning of antiphons and at the

[1] *Gregorian Chant*, (Bloomington, 1958), 255.
[2] *La Melopée antique dans le chant* (Gand, 1895), 235 ff.
[3] *Op. cit.*, 262.

142

beginnings of interior phrases. Another figure occurs as the intonation for most of the second mode (protus plagus) pieces: a c′ d′, or a prothetic variant such as d′ d′ a c′ d′:

Ex. 57.

This may occur within as well as at the beginning of second mode pieces. The number of antiphons related by these opening themes is not large; and in most cases the resemblance does not extend past the first few notes.

When it comes to cadences the antiphons show a greater uniformity. There is one figure which is very common at interior and final cadences. Here are a few of its forms on d′:

Ex. 58.

This cadence occurs as well on a′ and c′, and frequently, but without the quilisma, on f′and g′. On e′ it is rare; even so, two deuterus antiphons close:

Ex. 59.

Forty-nine of the one hundred and eleven antiphons end with this formula, and this number might be higher but for the Alleluias, which probably caused the modification of the final notes of some of the melodies.

Another figure is employed to conclude more than half of the deuterus pieces:

In most of these antiphons, however, the similarity goes beyond the last few notes and will be discussed below.

It might be best to include here, briefly, something about the most basic aspect of the cadences. The last note of internal phrases and the last note of the antiphons proper (not the Alleluias) is approached by the intervals of the descending second, ascending second, and descending third—this being the order of their frequency. The first, the descending second, occurs in nearly ninety percent of the cases.

More extensive relationships between the rogation antiphons are also to be found, mostly involving the opening and closing sections of the pieces. In the first example below, the two melodies are largely the same:

Ex. 61.

Source 23, folio 134v.

Source 23, folio 139.

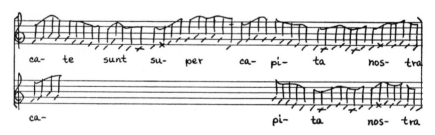

Ex. 61. (continued).

The following antiphons have similar beginnings, and in a few cases, other related passages:

Ex. 62.

Source 23, folio 134v.

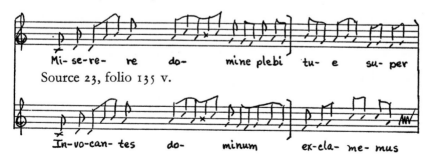

Source 23, folio 135 v.

Ex. 62. (continued).

Source 23, folio 135.

Source 23, folio 139v.

Source 33, folio 253v.

Ex. 63. The continuation of *Miserere Domine plebi* and a later passage of *Invocantes Dominum*.

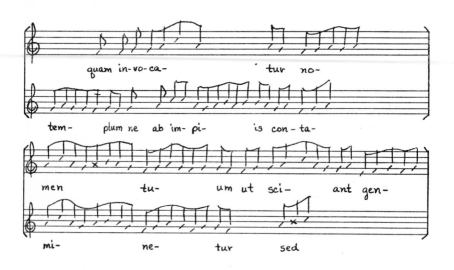

Ex. 64.[1]

Source 26, folio 164v.

Di-mitte domi-ne pec-ca-ta po- pu-li tu- i

Source 23, folio 135v.

Di-mitte do-mi-ne pecca- ta nos- tra

Ex. 65.

Source 23, folio 134.

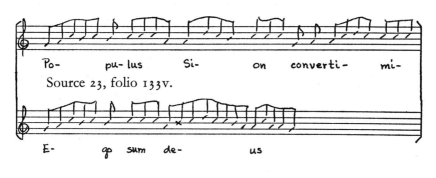

Po- pu-lus Si- on converti- mi-

Source 23, folio 133v.

E- go sum de- us

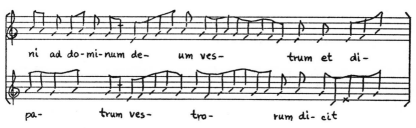

ni ad do-mi-num de- um ves- trum et di-

pa- trum ves- tro- rum di- cit

[1] Both these pieces begin on F in the Worcester Antiphoner (folio 229, source 46); the first ends on D, the second on F. Both end on D in the St. Yrieix Gradual (source 23, folio 134v, folio 135v).

Ex. 66. Source 23, folios 138v, 137v, 138v, 135v, 134v, 64, 139.

Ex. 67.

Source 23, folio 139v

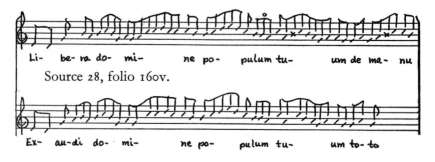

Source 28, folio 160v.

Source 23, folio 138v.

Ex-au-di do- mi- ne po- pulum tu- um confiten-tem

Source 23, folio 138v.

Res- pi-ce do- mi- ne quia a- ru- it ter- ra

Ex. 68.

Source 23, folio 139v.

Non nos de-mergat domi- ne tempestas a- que ne- que

Source 23, folio 138v.

Plate- e Jerusalem gaude- bunt et omnes

Source 23, folio 139.

Do- mi- ne ri-gans montes

Source 23, folio 134.

Confi-te - mi-ni do- mi-ne ..... Israel qui-a non est

Source 23, folio 138v.

Cus-todit do- mi- nus a-ni-mas

Ex. 69. Later passages of *Domine rigans*, *Confitemini* and *Custodit*.

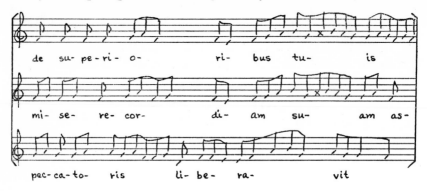

Ex. 70.

Source 23, folio 64.

Source 23, folio 134.

Ex. 71.

Source 26, folio 177.

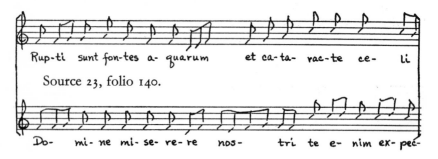

Source 23, folio 140.

a- per- te   sunt   in   gra- va- te sunt plu- vi- e

ta- mus   es- to bra-chi- um nos- trum

Ex. 72.

Source 23, folio 144.

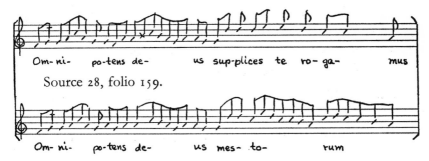

Om- ni- po-tens de-   us sup-plices te ro- ga-   mus

Source 28, folio 159.

Om- ni- po-tens de-   us mes- to-   rum

The first two antiphons of Ex. 62 are related at the close:

Ex. 73. The remainder of *Miserere Domine plebi,* and the conclusion of *Invocantes Dominum,* (*loc. cit*).

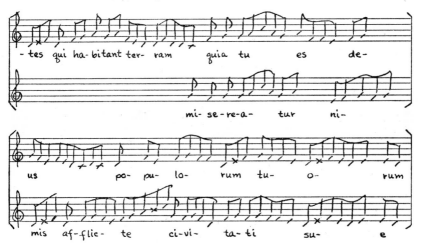

- tes qui ha- bi-tant ter- ram   quia tu   es   de-

mi- se- re- a-   tur   ni-

us   po- pu- lo-   rum tu-   o-   rum

mis af-flic- te   ci-vi-   ta- ti   su-   e

Ex. 74.

Similar endings are employed by several of the antiphons of Ex. 66 and 67, not necessarily those which open alike:

Respice domine

quod planta- vit dex- te- ra tu- a.

Exaudi domine lacrimas

quod plantavit dextera tu- a do- mi- ne de- us nos- ter.

Exaudi domine deprecationem servorum

sanctificationi tue do-mine de- us nos- ter.

Iuxta vestibulum

(internal cadence) et di- cent

Libera domine populum

benedicamus te do-mi-ne de- us nos- ter.

Exaudi domine populum tuum

dedisti patribus do-mine de- us nos- ter.

Exaudi domine populum tuum toto

restantes dex- tera tu- a do- mi- ne de- us nos- ter.

The loss of a third of the melodies makes it difficult to estimate the extent of musical relationships between the antiphons. It is to be supposed that textual parallels in some of the pieces whose music has not survived indicate at least some relationships now impossible to ascertain. In this respect, however, it is interesting to note that the musical similarity in the first, second and last antiphons of Ex. 74 does not cover all the words in common. As far as the surviving melodies are concerned it can be said that the antiphons are related only to others of the same mode, and that in some cases the musical correspondence seems to have been prompted by the text. Otherwise much of the similarity between antiphons seems haphazard.

It is unlikely, even if all the melodies were available for study, that any system would emerge which would explain all the melodic borrowings encountered. Possibly those antiphons which share a significant amount of musical material were at one time sung to the same melody. A practice like this —and perhaps an ancient vestige—seems to be indicated in the seven oldest manuscripts of the Pontifical of the *Roman Curia*. In these books one melody is prescribed for the three antiphons, *Ambulate sancti*, *Ecce populus*, and *Cum iocunditate*.[1] In other books these pieces have melodies which are not related.

THE ROGATION ANTIPHONS AND THE CHANTS OF THE MASS AND OFFICE

The manuscripts refer to the rogation pieces as antiphons,[2] and there seems little reason to dispute this designation.[3] The pieces do approach the responds of Matins in length and in the ornateness of their musical setting, but there is only a superficial resemblance. Other considerations

---

[1] The melody is that of *Ecce populus* in the Old Roman tradition (source 30). See Huglo "Les antiennes de la procession des reliques: Vestiges du chant 'Vieux Roman' dans le Pontifical" in *Revue Grégorienne*, 1952, p. 136.

[2] The only exception is *Rogamus te*. The Nonantola Troper (source 26) refers to this as a respond, and designates the latter portion as "verse." Musically there is a certain resemblance to the most common melody-type of the second mode Matins responds; the verse setting is free, and not according to the standard tone. The piece may be borrowed from an Office not current in any of the surviving service books. The question of processional responds is discussed further below.

[3] Peter Wagner, in a very brief discussion of these pieces (*Einführung in die Gregorianischen Melodien* [third edition, Leipzig, 1911], I, 158) remarks:

Das diesen Gesängen die Bezeichnung "Antiphone" nur im uneigentlichen Sinne zukommt, ergibt sich schon aus ihren Texten: sie haben fast alle die Form einer Oratio.

show unmistakably that the rogation pieces belong to the Antiphon category of chants. First is their association with psalm recitation.

In sources dating from about 800 to 1100, a period when a great many rogation antiphons were in use, psalm verses are prescribed for only a few of the shorter pieces. The following list is probably complete:

Ambulabunt sancti
Exaudi nos Domine quoniam
Exurge Domine adiuva

Exurge libera nos
Propitius esto
Sanctus Deus sanctus fortis
Sint occuli tui
Sub altare.

From contemporary descriptions of the ceremonies it seems clear that the recitation of psalms remained nevertheless a feature of the processions.[1]

In early times, when the distances they covered were customarily sizable, psalm-singing probably constituted a large proportion of the accompanying chants. Psalms figure prominently in the first notices of the rogations. At that time rogation antiphons were likely sung in the same manner as the antiphons of the Office, that is, before and after each psalm, or even between verses. Later, perhaps because there came to be so many antiphons, because they acquired a more elaborate setting, or because the route of the processions was shortened, the antiphons were sung with only one verse of a psalm, as is presently the Introit of the Mass, or alone, as are the Offertory and Communion. In the later Middle Ages, when the repertory was thinned out, the surviving processional antiphons came again to have association with psalms. All but one of the rogation pieces in the Sarum Processional have psalm verses indicated.

There are musical features which demonstrate further the affiliation of the rogation pieces with antiphons. The most obvious is the style of the verses—simple recitational settings, unlike the elaborated melodies of those of the responds. Next is the attitude to the accentuation of the Latin. It has been noted that in the processional pieces the melismas tend to occur on the accented syllables of words. An exhaustive statistical tabulation[2] has shown that antiphons tend to respect the text accent with a melismatic, sustaining accent, and that the responsorial chants are clearly indifferent towards it. One final consideration is that the pro-

---

[1] Sources 2, 9, and 20.
[2] Apel, *op. cit.*, 275-300.

cessionals do not make use of melody-types as do the responds of Matins, the *responsoria brevia* of the lesser hours, and the Graduals of the Mass. Certainly if such a procedure were operating in the rogation pieces it would be apparent in a body as large as that which survives. Curiously, the rogation chant *Domine rex omnipotens* opens like a typical second mode Matins respond. But it is clear that this is simply a case of borrowing a fragment of a well-known melody for similar text. Following is the beginning of the antiphon and the opening of a respond sung at Sarum (and elsewhere) at Matins during the *historia Judith*:

Ex. 75.

Antiphonale Sarisburiense (ed. cit.) p. 321.

Resp.

Source 28, folio 160v.

Ant.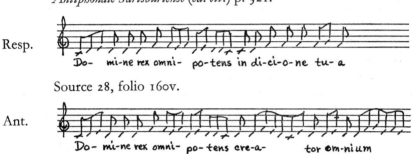

The antiphons for the rogation processions resemble in certain aspects both the antiphons of the Office and those of the Mass, and incline clearly to neither. The simplest of the rogation pieces would be indistinguishable from the psalmodic antiphons of the Office. But the typical processional chants are longer and more ornate, surpassing in this respect even the Magnificat and Benedictus antiphons, and standing closer to the antiphons of the Mass. A general similarity of style between the rogation and Mass pieces is rather to be expected, considering that the liturgical function was the same. The Mass antiphons themselves accompany, or at one time did accompany, actions which might loosely be described as processions.[1] In the detail of melodic design, and as regards the great variation in their length and style, the rogation pieces most closely resemble the Offertories, although these, the most ornate of all the antiphons of the Liturgy, are on the whole more flamboyant.

Certain features in common, viz frequent psalm-tone reminiscences,

---

[1] For the early functions of the Mass chants, see Jacques Froger, *Les chants de la Messe aux VIIIe et IXe Sièles* (Paris, 1950).

short syllabic passages on one pitch, and the prominence of *strophici* suggest a kinship to the Introits. But there may be a simpler explanation. These characteristics have given rise to a theory that the Introits "were simple recitatives ... which in the course of time became considerably more florid."[1] The same arguments would apply to the rogation pieces, which have the same features; and a parallel development from simple recitation would make less significant what appear at first to be striking similarities between the processional chants and the Mass antiphons.

The verse settings for the processional pieces, where these are indicated, seem to be according to the tones in use for the verses of the Introits, Communions and Magnificat—not according to the tones of the psalmodic antiphons of the Office. However the evidence on this point is scanty; and there exists the possibility that in the late restoration of the psalm verses to the processional pieces—as at Sarum—the ancient practice did not survive.

In other respects there seems to be an affinity between the rogation antiphons and those of the Office. Both have texts partly or wholly original; both, when they do borrow, borrow from a variety of sources. The Mass antiphons are almost entirely psalmodic. Both Office and rogation antiphons show the same modal distribution: a decided preference for the protus and tetrardus *maneriae*, and a disinclination to the tritus. Offertories, Communions, and especially Introits are distributed much more evenly.

The themes of the Office antiphons, which have been listed by Gevaert in his famous study, do not operate in the rogation pieces. There are, of course, resemblances: the two recurring first mode intonation figures discussed above form the beginning of Gevaert's *theme 3, 4* and *6*.[2] But similarities between the incipits of processional antiphons and Mass pieces can just as easily be adduced.

THE AGE AND PROVENANCE OF THE REPERTORY

It is unlikely that any special chants existed for the "sporadic, unenthusiastic, infrequent, and uninteresting"[3] rogation processions which existed before the institution of the Rogation Days at the end of the fifth century. Fortunatus, writing, probably, in the latter part of the

[1] Apel, *op. cit.*, 307-309.
[2] *Op. cit.*, 235 ff.
[3] Sidonius Apollinaris, *loc. cit.*

sixth century, mentions only "psalm singers" in the processions,[1] but special antiphons for the psalms—that is to say the rogation antiphons—were probably already current.

The Venerable Bede reports that the missionaries sent to England by Pope Gregory I sang, on their arrival in the year 596, an antiphon, *Deprecamur te domine*:

Fertur autem quia adpropinquantes civitati, more suo cum cruce sancta, et imagine magni regis Domini nostri Jesu Christi, hanc letaniam consona voce modularentur: "Deprecamur te Domine, in omni misericordia tua, ut auferatur furor tuus et ira tua a civitate ista, et de domo sanctua tua, quoniam peccavimus. Alleluia."[2]	As they approached the city, bearing the holy cross and the likeness of our great King and Lord Jesus Christ, they sang together as was their custom this litany: "We pray, Lord, that in all your mercy your wrath and anger may be averted from this city and from your holy house, for we have sinned. Alleluia."

The text of this piece is the same as that of the Gregorian rogation chant. Without insisting that the melody remained unchanged over several centuries, it seems clear that Bede was actually referring to the Gregorian antiphon. The text is a free composition, not a scriptural quotation, and a fortuitous verbatim correspondence is out of the question.

There is evidence almost as early for several other antiphons. The following:

Cum iocunditate
De Jerusalem
In Niniven
In Nomine domini
Numquid est in idolis
Numquid valet manus
Populus Sion
Signum salutis

are found in the León Gradual, a manuscript which contains chants in use in the late seventh century.[3] For these pieces as well—again with a qualification about their melodies—identification is established by the almost exact correspondence of the texts in the Gregorian and Visigothic sources.

As far as the stylistic features of the Gregorian versions are concerned there is nothing to distinguish *Deprecamur te* or any of the eight in the

[1] *Loc. cit.*
[2] *PL*, XCV, 56.
[3] See the commentary to source 1.

Visigothic book from the great majority of the rogation antiphons. It seems almost certain that most existed long before their first appearance in the service books of the ninth century. All this has not been to insist that there were no later additions to the repertory of rogation antiphons. Unusual features—the low f, and leaps of a sixth in the melodies—set apart the following pieces, none of which are in the earliest manuscripts:

Ex. 76. *Sicut pastor portat*, Source 23, folio 144v.

Ex. 77. *Domine Deus omnipotens*, Source 57, folio 86.

Ex. 78. *Respice cuncta*, Source 28, folio 160v.

Ex. 79. *Si clauso celo*, Source 23, folio 139.

Such exceptional features are, however, confined to these few antiphons. It has been suggested[1] that the low g indicates chants of later composition. This idea does not seem well founded, but in any case, as was noted earlier, only four of the rogation antiphons descend to this note, and one of them, *Sicut pastor*, with its low f, has already been counted.

[1] Apel, *op. cit.*, 248.

At this point it is necessary to consider briefly the provenance of these antiphons under study. It is not enough to say "Gregorian" for chants which existed before this rite took form. The Gregorian Corpus as a whole consists of a Roman nucleus with additions, mainly Gallican, acquired when it was brought in by the first Carolingian monarchs to supplant the native rite. This, in all probability, is the constitution of the repertory for the rogation processions as well: the Roman chants for the procession on St. Mark's Day supplemented by Gallican and other pieces for the Rogation Days. Any stylistic differences between the Roman, Gallican and other pieces would have been obliterated by the musical revision undertaken during the period from 750 to 850, a revision generally believed to have given the chants the musical form which characterizes them as Gregorian.

The bulk of the Roman contribution is probably the repertory contained in the Old Roman books. Two of them[1] contain versions of about fifty of the Gregorian antiphons.[2] There is no hope of settling here the controversy on this question; but it is widely accepted that these manuscripts, although relatively recent, contain Roman chants which have not undergone the Gregorian revision. The evidence of the rogation antiphons does seem to support those who maintain that the contents of these manuscripts represent a very early period: they provide the only concordances for a number of the processional antiphons in the very oldest Gregorian and other manuscripts. It should be said that the rogation antiphons in the Old Roman books could not be late additions of Gregorian origin. The melodies, although almost always recognizable, are obviously of a different tradition. Compare the two versions of the first part of *Domine Deus noster*:

Ex. 80.

Source 23, folio 134.

Do- mi- ne de- us nos- ter

Source 30, folio 101 (Old Roman).

---

[1] Sources 30, 62.
[2] Only a handful of the antiphons in the Old Roman books cannot be found in Gregorian sources.

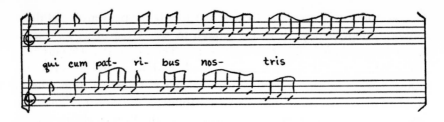

qui cum pat- ri- bus nos- tris

In some cases the versions are closer. A few antiphons have what appear to be partly or entirely different melodies in the Old Roman and Gregorian books. It is sometimes difficult to decide, but the following, at least, are examples:

Domine iminuti sumus
Domine miserere nostri
Ecce populus custodiens
Recordare Domine.

Some of the characteristics which distinguish the Old Roman Mass pieces are also present in the Old Roman processional antiphons. It has been observed, for example, that "the antiphons [Introits] are more ornate than the Gregorian in their neumatic passages, and more barren in their syllabic sections."[1] With this in mind compare the opening of *Ambulate sancti dei ad locum* in both versions:

Ex. 81.

Source 30, folio 135v.

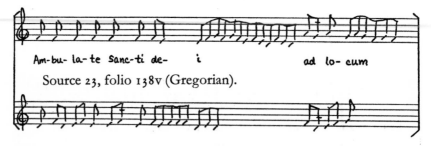

Am-bu- la- te Sanc-ti de- i   ad lo- cum

Source 23, folio 138v (Gregorian).

It is almost certain that the Gregorian rogation antiphons include some—perhaps a large number—of Gallican origin. It can be assumed, in spite of the fact that none of the ancient Frankish books survive, that there was a body of Gallican pieces. The evidence is circumstantial. The Rogation

[1] R. J. Snow, "The Old Roman Chant," in Apel, *op. cit.*, 487.

Days originated in Frankish territory and would have been provided for there at least as well as elsewhere. And large and almost independent repertories of chants for the rogation processions existed for both the neighbouring Spanish and Milanese rites. The León Gradual and the Trivulziana Codex[1] each contain seventy or so pieces similar in appearance to the Gregorian. Following are a few of the incipits:

(Visigothic)
    Orate sacerdotes et plorate
    Jerusalem plorans plorabit
    In fuore tuo Domine
    Aperi celos tuos
    Dimitte obsecro peccata

(Milanese)
    Peccavimus ante te
    Dies tribulationis
    Domine non sumus digni
    In tribulatione nostra
    Non est aliud refugium.

There is no question that the León manuscript is purely Visigothic. The Milanese manuscript is relatively recent and contains Gregorian influences, but there can be little doubt that the great majority of the rogation antiphons belong to the ancient tradition. The occasions for the processions (the three days *after* Ascension) are specifically Milanese, and almost all the chants are unknown elsewhere.

The concordances in the Milanese and Visigothic books may indicate that a few of the Gregorian antiphons were taken over from these rites. It is just as possible, however, that these pieces were Gallican. A close association is known to have existed between the Frankish, Spanish, and Milanese Churches.[2]

An Italian provenance not specifically Roman is indicated for twenty-five of the antiphons, for their distribution is confined to peninsular sources. These pieces are not very different from the others. Sixteen of the twenty-one melodies which can be transcribed are noticeably simpler in style, with fewer, and mostly shorter melismas. More than half are in the G mode. (The Italian preference for the higher modes has already been noted.)

Two antiphons in the Nonantola Troper,[3] *Peccavimus Domine peccavimus* and *Dimitte Domine peccata*, and two others in the Beneventan Gradual,[4]

---

[1] Source 1, 35.
[2] Duchesne, *op. cit.*, III.
[3] Source 26, folio 177v, 164v.
[4] Source 30 folio, 141.

Miserere Domine plebi and *Non nos demergat,* do not use the Gregorian melodies. A similar situation has been observed in the case of some of the antiphons in the Old Roman books, but it cannot be supposed that there was a single, independent Italian tradition: *Miserere Domine plebi,* in the Roman source, is set to the usual Gregorian melody.[1] A very few other antiphons appear only in Aquitainian, Aquitainian and Italian, or in German sources. There is nothing stylistically to distinguish these chants from the others.

Some of the regional chants may be later compositions, but this must not be inferred from the date of the manuscripts in which they first appear. In most cases they are the earliest sources of the region.

As many as forty antiphons, almost a quarter of the total, seem from the manuscripts at hand to have been current only in the northern part of France. But it must be borne in mind that the two sources chiefly involved, the Compiègne and Senlis graduals,[2] are among the very oldest to survive and may simply preserve antiphons which at a later date had fallen out of general use. The decay of the repertory had probably begun by the ninth century. The later books of the same region omit these pieces.

---

[1] Source 28, folio 161, 159v.   [2] Sources 4 and 6.

X. THE SPECIAL CHANTS
2. THE PIECES FOR SUNDAY
AND FESTAL PROCESSIONS

At Sarum and generally in the later Middle Ages, Office chants served for ordinary Sunday processions. In earlier manuscripts rogation antiphons or lenten processional pieces are sometimes prescribed.[1] It has already been suggested that this might be the meaning of rubrics such as "de cruce," "ad crucem deducendam," etc. A few sources of the tenth and eleventh centuries provide collections of chants to be used in the processions "for Sundays" (Novalesa); for "the Sundays after Pentecost" (St. Yrieix and probably Chartres);[2] or more specifically "de Tobi," "de Regum," etc.—that is, for the (summer) periods while the Matins lections were drawn from these books of the Old Testament (St. Martial, Limoges).[3] Most of these pieces can be traced to the Office; frequently they are antiphons for the Magnificat and Benedictus. A few may actually be special pieces, but none had more than local usage.

For the Sundays of the two penitential seasons, that is, in Advent and from Septuagesima through Lent, the Sarum Processional included four special antiphons:

> Missus est Angelus
> Cum venerimus ante conspectum
> Ecce carissimi dies illa
> In die quando venerit.

The first, *Missus est Angelus*, was customary for Advent throughout England, and not only in churches which followed the Sarum Rite. It was the choice in some churches on the Continent,[4] but there it was nowhere near as popular. *Ecce carissimi* is the only other processional antiphon which seems to have had any widespread currency for Advent.[5]

Missus est, although not used otherwise at Sarum, is not originally a

---

[1] Sources 12, 23, 26 and 27.
[2] Sources 27, 23, 10; see *Paléographie Musicale*, XI, 271.
[3] Sources 16 and 17.
[4] As in Rouen and Limoges, sources 11, 16, 57.
[5] It is specified in books from Louvain, Metz, and Toulouse (sources 102, 54, 34).

processional chant but one of the great Marian Antiphons. It is listed with others of its type (which included *O Maria Iesse virgo, Gaude Dei Genetrix*, and *Beata es virgo*) in the books of a number of churches. Its text is a precis of the Luke I, 26-38 Gospel account of the Annunciation, and this has made it especially appropriate to Advent, whose liturgical theme is the expectation of the Incarnation.

For the Sunday processions of the lenten season the service books of the tenth and eleventh centuries provided six pieces: the three Sarum chants (*Cum venerimus, Ecce carissimi, In die quando*) plus:

> Christe pater misericordiarum
> Cum sederit filius
> Memor humane conditionis.

Later manuscripts usually include one or more of this group in their chants for this procession.

All six of these pieces are referred to as antiphons by the rubrics. Nevertheless, it seems better to call *Ecce carissimi* a respond: it is melismatic, it has an elaborate verse and the typical form, with the latter part of the respond repeated after the verse. This chant, although it does not use one of the standard melodies, might easily be taken for an ordinary second mode Matins respond. The melody does not exceed a fifth (cf. the responds *Ingrediente Domino, Domine Rex omnipotens*[1]), and there is a typical responsorial *neuma* at the close, longer than the others, and with the familiar structure AAB:

Ex. 82. Ms Rawl. lit. d. 4, folio 21.

sum et possi-de-a- tis reg-

na ce- lo- rum.

The verse has a free setting scarcely less elaborate than the respond.

The five antiphons resemble the more elaborate rogation pieces,

---

[1] *Antiphonale Sarisburiense (ed. cit.)* p. 205, 321.

except that the melismas tend to be longer. Two of the antiphons end with groups reminiscent of the responsorial *neumata*:

Ex. 83. From *Cum venerimus*, Ms Rawl. lit. d. 4, folio 31.

e- ter- nita-   tis   reg- na.

Ex. 84. From *Cum sederit*, Source 23, folio 70.

in se-   cu-   la.

The texts of the pieces are prose; none are scriptural quotations. *Memor humane* and *Christe pater* are penitential in character, and seek God's mercy; the others, including *Ecce carissimi*, are quasi-prophetic, and describe the Day of Judgement.

These pieces are absent from the earliest service books. *Ecce carissimi* is found first in the Laon Gradual, written about the year 900.[1] The earliest appearance of the five others is about a hundred years later, in manuscripts from Limoges.[2]

FESTAL PROCESSIONS

For the Candlemas procession at Sarum there were three special antiphons: *Adorna thalamum*, *Responsum accepit*, and *Ave gratia plena*. These seem to have been sung everywhere from the first appearance of the procession. Two other pieces, apparently special processional antiphons, appear locally—one, *Ecce Maria venit*, in the eleventh century St. Yrieix Gradual; the other, *Suscipiens Jesum in ulnis*, in the ninth century Compiègne Gradual.[3] These pieces are always referred to as antiphons. Sometimes, however, as at St. Yrieix and Sarum, *Responsum* has a verse "Hodie beata virgo." In these places the piece was sung as a respond, with the last part of the antiphon repeated after the verse. (This "Hodie

[1] Source 8.
[2] Sources 11, 16, 17.
[3] Sources 23 and 4.

beata virgo" appears separately in a processional from Metz.)[1] Similarly, *Adorna thalamum* was sung with the verse "Accipiens eus Symeon" in churches following the Use of York.[2]

The texts of the five antiphons refer to the events of Luke II, 26 ff., the presentation by Mary of the infant Jesus at the Temple. *Adorna* and *Ave gratia* are paeans to the Virgin, the others are narrative. The text of *Responsum*, drawn entirely from the Gospel, is a precis of Luke II, 26-29. The two Marian hymns are Latin versions of Byzantine texts: *Adorna thalamum* of the sticheron, *Cathacosmyso*, and *Ave gratia plena* of *Chaere cecaritomeni*. Both Greek and Latin texts are provided for these pieces in the eighth-century Gradual of Mont-Blandin.[3] *Suscipiens Jesum in ulnis* has the same text as the opening of a Matins respond for the Feast of the Purification. These processional pieces are modest in character and contain nothing un-Gregorian in their melodic progressions. *Adorna* and *Responsum*, however, make extensive use of repetition. For the eight main divisions of the text of the first piece the musical material is repeated in the pattern AABBCDDE. The first two sections use the same music exactly; in the others it is the beginnings of the melodies which correspond. Two cadential melodic figures each appear twice. The melody of *Responsum*, which is not a long piece, uses two cadential figures, each three times, and one opening figure twice.

These characteristics may indicate—as has been widely suggested— that *Adorna* and *Responsum* have Byzantine melodies. But the late date of their composition—the Feast was not introduced in the West until the eighth century—would also explain their unusual design. Two things should be noted in this respect: that there is nothing unusual about the melody for *Ave gratia plena*, whose text is certainly Greek, and that there is no evidence that *Responsum*—with its repeated melodic figures—is not originally Latin.

For Palm Sunday at Sarum there were seven processional antiphons and a special respond. In other churches the ceremonies for this occasion varied considerably and required more or fewer chants. The earliest sources together contain some eighteen antiphons and responds for the Palm Sunday procession.[4]

---

[1] Source 54.

[2] Source 73.

[3] Source 3.

[4] Two other pieces, *Dum fabricator* and *Cum rex gloria*, are given occasionally for this procession. Usually however they are included with the Easter pieces, and as their texts are more appropriate for this occasion they have been considered Easter chants.

Table 2

The distribution of Palm Sunday pieces in sixteen of the oldest chant sources

	Compiègne (4) (IX)	Laon (8) (IX-X)	Chartres (10) (X)	Mont-Renaud (12) (X)	Limoges (11) (X)	Limoges (17) (X-XI)	St. Yrieix (23) (XI)	Montpellier (18) (X-XI)	Mainz (13) (X)	St. Gall (15) (X)	St. Gall (14) (X)	Einsiedeln (19) (X-XI)	Novalesa (27) (XI)	Benevento (28) (XI-XII)	León (1)	Rome (30)
Ante sex dies passionis ⎫ Ante sex dies sollenitatis ⎭	x	x	x	x		x		x	x			x		x		
Appropinquante Jesu filio	x				x	x	x	x					x			
Ave rex noster			x		x	x	x						x			
Ceperunt omnes turba	x	x	x		x	x	x	x	x		x			x		
Collegerunt pontifices v. Unus autem	x	x	x	x	x	x	x	x	x	x	x	x	x	x		
Cum appropinquaret	x	x	x	x	x	x	x	x	x	x	x	x	x	x	x	
Cum audisset	x	x	x	x	x	x	x	x	x	x	x	x	x	x		
Fulgentibus palmis												x				
Hosanna filio David									x		x	x				x
Insignes[1]									x							
Introeuntem te domine					x	x	x									
Multa turba iudeorum							x	x								
Occurunt turbe					x	x	x	x	x				x	x		x
Prima autem azimorum						x		x								
Salvator unigeniti	x															
Scriptum est enim[2]									x							
Turba multa[3] ps. Cantate									x							
(the Sarum pieces are marked*)																

Collegerunt pontifices, although sometimes labelled "antiphon" in the manuscripts, is usually listed with the responds in modern collections—perhaps because it has an elaborate verse and employs the usual responsorial repeat pattern. Actually it stands apart from both classes of chant. Its melody features striking boldness of design, long melismas, large leaps, and a wide range:

[1] This may be *Insignes preconiis* the Office antiphon.
[2] This is listed in the tonary of Regino of Prüm (d. 915).
[3] Perhaps the same piece as the *Turba multa* in the *Liber Usualis* (p. 588).

Ex. 85. Ms Rawl. lit. d. 4, folio 48.

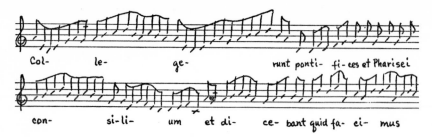

The verse is very elaborate and employs musical material from the respond. Compare the opening of the verse of this piece with the music of "Collegerunt" above:

Ex. 86.

The following are related passages (a) from the respond, and (b) from the verse:

Ex. 87.

The text of respond and verse is scriptural, from John's account (XI, 46-51) of the plot of the Priests and Pharisees to kill Jesus, and sets the tone of foreboding underlying the festive events commemorated on Palm Sunday.

The antiphons for Palm Sunday, those whose melodies survive, share

certain of the musical features of the rogation chants. The tunes fall
into sections, corresponding to text phrases, which begin frequently with
the same intonation figure; often they contain reminiscences of psalm-
tones or passages of recitation on one pitch; *strophici* are numerous.
(These features are not found in *Collegerunt*.) Five antiphons:

> Ante sex dies passionis
> Ante sex dies sollenitatis
> Cum appropinquaret
> Cum audisset
> Prima autem azimorum

are flamboyant, with striking or angular melodic design and melismas of
up to twenty notes:

Ex. 88. *Ante sex dies passionis*, Ms Rawl. lit. d. 4, folio 44.

Ex. 89. *Cum appropinquaret*, Ms Rawl. lit. d. 4, folio 42.

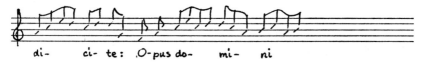

Ex. 90. *Cum audisset*, Ms Rawl. lit. d. 4, folio 43.

Ex. 91. *Prima autem azimorum*, Ms Rawl. lit. d. 4, folio 41v.

The two antiphons *Ante sex dies* have much of their text and music in common.

About half of the surviving melodies are simpler and might, except for their texts, be taken for rogation pieces or Office antiphons. *Multa turba*, in fact, opens with the same melody as *Pueri hebreorum*, an antiphon for the lesser Hours on Palm Sunday:

Ex. 92.

Source 23, folio 120.

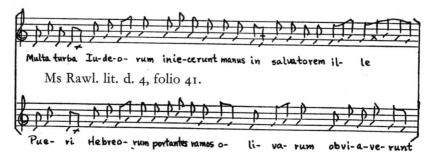

Multa turba Iu-de-o- rum inie-cerunt manus in salvatorem il- le

Ms Rawl. lit. d. 4, folio 41.

Pue- ri Hebreo- rum portantes ramos o- li- va- rum obvi-a-ve-runt

For two of the antiphons, *Insignes* and *Scriptum est*, only text cues survive. The second of these may be *Insignes preconiis*, a festive Office antiphon prescribed for more than one occasion in medieval books.[1] All but two of the others refer to Christ's triumphal entry into Jerusalem. Two texts are scriptural: *Prima autem* is taken from Matthew XXV, 17 ff.; *Ceperunt omnes*, from Luke XIX, 37-39. The others are paraphrases of the Gospels and borrow phrases freely from Matthew XX, 1-9; Mark XI, 1-10; Luke XIX, 29-38; and John XII, 1-13.

The antiphon *Salvator* is very short and perhaps originally an Office piece. Its text is not particularly appropriate for Palm Sunday: "Salvator unigeniti qui nos venisti redimere gloria tibi Christe redemptor (Only-begotten Saviour who came to redeem us, glory to you Christ our Redeemer.). *Multa turba* refers to the crucifixion, and seems quite out of place for this occasion. The fact that it shares the melody of a well-known Palm Sunday chant may account for its appearance.

The Palm Sunday processional chants may be late. The special procession with palms is not mentioned in Roman or Frankish sources before the eighth century. It was, however, the custom much earlier in

[1] For the Feast of St. Michael at Mont-Rénaud, for St. Denis at Hereford (source 12; indices to the Hereford Breviary, *Publications of the Henry Bradshaw Society*, XLVI).

Jerusalem and the East and in the Visigothic Rite, which may have introduced the practice into the West.[1] One of the antiphons for the Gregorian procession may have come from the Visigothic books. *Cum appropinquaret* is found among the chants for the Palm Sunday procession in the Antiphoner of León, whose contents may be supposed to antedate the adoption of the custom in the Latin churches outside of Spain. The identity of the piece is established in this case by the text— a free biblical paraphrase, not a scriptural quotation. It is difficult to say anything about the Spanish melody, which survives only in cheironomic neumes; but it is in the same ornate style as the Gregorian, and seems to begin similarly:

Ex. 93.

Source 1, folio 153v (Visigothic).

Ms Rawl. lit. d. 4., folio 42.

Cum   ap- pro- pin-   quaret   do-

For Easter at Sarum there were five special processional antiphons or responds. In other churches, just as for Palm Sunday, the ceremonies, and therefore the number of chants, varied considerably. Easter processional pieces are found in the oldest sources; those of the ninth to the eleventh century contain, altogether, some eighteen, listed in the following table. Of this number the seven or eight which were most widespread were customary in the later Middle Ages. The Sarum pieces are indicated by an asterisk. For seven of these antiphons, those marked with a cross, the melodies are lost; for *Surrexit Dominus* only a text cue survives.

[1] See the discussion of the processional customs.

Table 3

The distribution of the Easter chants in sixteen of the oldest sources

	(IX)	(IX)	(IX-X)	(X)	(X)	(X)	(X-XI)	(X-XI)	(XI)	(X)	(X)	(X)	(X-XI)	(XI)	(XI-XII)
	Compiègne (4)	Compiègne (5)	Laon (8)	Chartres (10)	Mont-Rénaud (12)	Limoges (11)	Limoges (16)	Limoges (17)	St. Yrieix (23)	Mainz (13)	St. Gall (15)	St. Gall (14)	Einsiedeln (19)	Novalesa (27)	Benevento (28)
+ Ait dominus Jesus														x	
* Christus resurgens v. Dicant nunc						x	x	x	x					x	
+ Christus surrexit														x	
Cum rex gloria			x								x	x		x	x
* Dum fabricator¹			x			x		x	x			x	x	x	
* Ego sum alpha et O							x	x	x			x	x	x	x
In die resurrectionis		x		x	x	x	x	x	x	x	x		x	x	
Longo contritus carcere	x								x						
+ Maria et Martha	x														
+ Maria vidit	x													x	
+ Populus ad qui											x				
Postquam resurrexit									x						
* Sedit² angelus v. Crucifixum	x			x		x	x	x	x	x	x	x	x	x	
+ Surrexit dominus						x									
Surrexit enim sicut				x		x	x	x			x	x	x		
Surrexit pastor						x	x	x							
Venit Maria Magdalene									x						
+ Venite omnes adoremus qui de morte														x	

The texts of these pieces are prose. None are scriptural quotations. One group is narrative and retells the events of the Resurrection. Some of these are biblical paraphrases: *Cum fabricator* of Matthew XVII, 50 ff., and Mark XV, 37 ff.; *Venit Maria, Maria et Martha,* and *Maria vidit,* of Matthew XXVIII, 1 ff., and Luke XXIV, 2 ff. Another group proclaims the Gospel message of the Resurrection.

A few of the texts are prophetic in tone and refer to the Day of Judgement; one, *Ego sum alpha,* employs apocalyptic phrases from Revelations I, XXI, XXII. Very similar texts reminiscent of the Prophets

---

¹ This often appears as "Cum fabricator."

² This can be found as "Stetit angelus," "Stabat angelus," etc.

and Revelations are used in the processional chants for the Rogations, the Septuagesima-Lent period, and for Easter:

Terribile est Christe iudicium tuum ubi cherubim et seraphim contremiscunt, ubi angeli tremunt qui non peccaverunt ...	Terrible, Christ, is your judgement, when cherubim and seraphim tremble, when angels who have sinned not shake in fear ...
Cum venerimus ante conspectum Domini in die iudicii ubi assistent millia millium et decies centena milia angelorum cherubim et seraphyn ...	When we come before the Lord on the Day of Judgement, when a thousand thousands, even ten times a hundred thousand angels, cherubim and seraphim ...
Cum rex gloria Christus infernum devellaturus intraret et chorus angeli eius ante faciem eius portas principium tollere preciperet...	When Christ the King of Glory storms hell and a chorus of angels bring before him the gates of its fastness ...

It is doubtful however that this indicates a significant relationship. Apocalyptic language appears frequently in the free chants and prayers of the Liturgy. Its importance in the processions for these three occasions is only in keeping with its special appropriateness.

As far as the melodies are concerned the repertory is like that for Palm Sunday. One group of antiphons, including *Christus resurgens, Cum fabricator, Stetit Angelus,* and *Venit Maria,* has striking melodies with frequent melismas, some of twenty notes and more:

Ex. 94. Part of *Cum fabricator* and the opening of its verse, Ms Rawl. lit. d. 4, folio 67v.

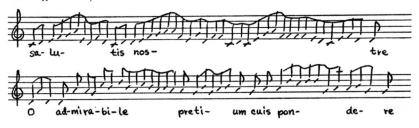

Ex. 95. From the verse of *Christus resurgens,* Ms Rawl. lit. d. 4, folio 86.

The other pieces are simpler, although those which are narratives are quite long. Except for their texts they could be taken for rogation antiphons.

The Easter processional pieces are usually designated as antiphons in the medieval service books. Four of them, however, *Ego sum alpha*, *Christus resurgens*, *Cum fabricator*, and *Sedit Angelus*, have the form of responds: elaborate verses and the usual repeat pattern. The responds and verses are similar in style and sometimes have musical material in common. In none of these are standard respond melodies or verse tones used.

The designation "respond" has been used for a number of the processional chants of the lenten period, for Palm Sunday, and for Easter. None has any responsorial function in connection with lections, and there is no indication that any were Office chants prior to their use in the processions. There is reason to think that the distinction between verse and respond and the practice with regard to the repeat were arbitrary. It may be best not to distinguish sharply between these and the other processional pieces. *Ego sum*, for example, might easily have been divided differently; several of its sections begin with the same intonation figure. This piece can, in fact, be found in other forms. The printed Sarum Processional of 1508 omits one of the phrases. The modern *Processionale Monasticum*[1] contains a much shortened version, called "antiphon", in which the section "Ego sum vestra redemtio," the verse at Sarum, is not set apart. There are other interesting cases. *Cum fabricator* is usually given with one verse, "O admirabile pretium"; but in the *Liturgicon* of Pamelius the text is divided again, at "aperto ergo," for a second verse. "Ecce mater nostra," usually the verse of *Ecce carissimi*, appears separately as an "antiphon" in a St. Martial troper.[2] In another St. Martial book[3] *Stabat* (usually "sedit") *Angelus* has no verse "Crucifixum in carne." But a cue to a separate piece "Crucifixum" is found among the Easter processional pieces in the Mont-Renaud manuscript.[4] Finally, the antiphon *Ave rex noster* has a "verse" *Ante sex dies* in a book from Novalesa.[5]

THE PROCESSIONAL HYMNS

There were three hymns sung in the processions at Sarum, one of them, *Salve festa dies*, frequently. The original version, speaking only for the text of course, is by Venantius Fortunatus (d. *circa* 600), but it was added

---

[1] Solesmes, 1893.

[2] Source 16.

[3] Source 15.

[4] Source 12.

[5] Source 27.

to greatly until it was, surely, the longest hymn of the Latin Church. Eight sets of verses were sung at Sarum for the great festivals of Easter, Ascension, Pentecost, Corpus Christi, Dedication, Visitation, Transfiguration, and the Feast of the Holy Name. This hymn was current on the Continent: it is found in processionals and other books from Pontetto (northern Italy), Rouen and Louvain.[1] In England, however, it was extremely popular and in some churches sung for many more occasions than at Sarum.[2]

The two other hymns were *En rex venit* and *Gloria laus et honor*, both for Palm Sunday. The first was widespread in England and can be found on the Continent in books from Rouen.[3] The second, by Theodulph, bishop of Orléans (d. 821), was, and is, universal.

All three pieces have the form peculiar to processional hymns: the verses are separated by repetitions of a refrain; refrain and verse are sung to different melodies.

---

[1] Sources 29, 56, 57 and 102.
[2] A processional from a church in Essex, source 84, includes versions for Christmas, Assumption, St. Ossith, Saints Peter and Paul, St. Augustine and others.
[3] Sources 56, 57, etc.

APPENDICES

Figure 2.   A Diagram of Sarum Cathedral.

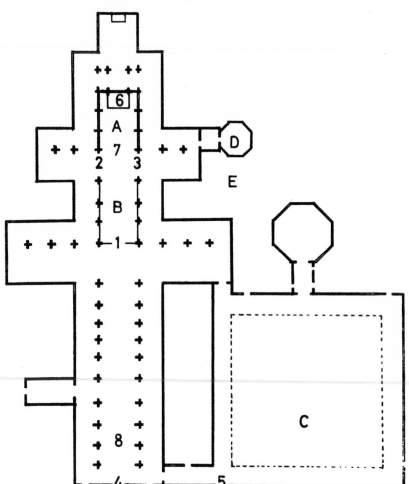

Presbytery	A	Western entrance to the church	4
Choir	B	Canons' Portal	5
Cloister	C	Main altar	6
Sacristy (vestibule)	D	Altar-step	7
Canons' Cemetery	E	Font	8
Western entrance to the choir	1	Choir-step	1
North entrance to the choir and presbytery	2	Pulpitum (the loft above the western entrance to the choir)	1
South entrance to the choir and presbytery	3	Rood (mounted on the pulpitum)	1

APPENDIX II

THE WOODCUTS ILLUSTRATING THE STATIONS WHICH APPEARED IN THE EDITIONS OF 1502 AND FOLLOWING[1]

Figure 3. The Sunday Blessing of the Holy Water.

[1] Reproduced from Henderson (*op. cit.*).

Figure 4. The Ejection of the Penitents on Ash Wednesday.

Figure 5. The Palm Sunday Blessing of the Branches.

Figure 6. The Holy Saturday Blessing of the New Fire.

Figure 7. The Holy Saturday Blessing of the Paschal Candle.

Figure 8. The Singing of the Litany at the Font on Holy Saturday.

Figure 9. The Station and Procession with the Cross on Easter before Matins.

Figure 10. The Station at the Font at Vespers during Easter Week.

Figure 11. The Procession for Rogation Monday.

Figure 12. The Station and Procession before Mass on Ascension.

Figure 13. The Station before the Cross at Vespers during the Summer.

Figure 14. The Blessing of the Candles on Purification.

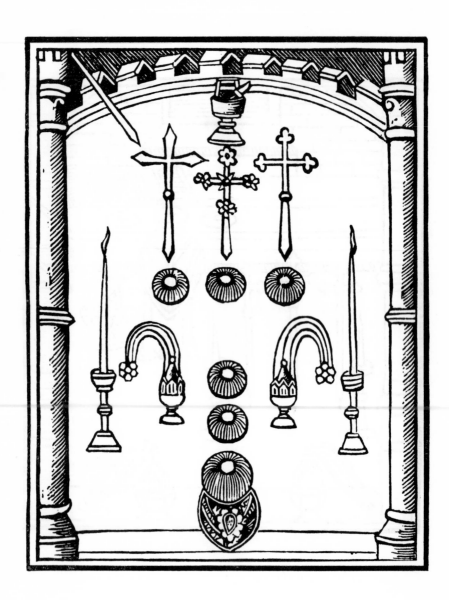

Figure 15. The Procession before Mass on Christmas.

MANUSCRIPTS CONSULTED

Autun,	Bibliothèque Municipale,	Ms 183.
		Ms 98 S.
		Ms 181 S.
Cambrai,	Bibliothèque Municipale,	Processional (no number).
Cambridge,	Caius College,	Ms 436.
	Fitzwilliam Library,	Ms James 42.
		Ms McClean 63.
	Jesus College,	Ms 62.
	St. John's College,	Ms 151.
		Ms 268.
		Ms F 2.
	University Library,	Ms addl. 5336.
		Ms Mm 2g.
Dublin,	Archbishop Marsh Library,	Ms Z 4.2.20.
Edinburgh,	National Library of Scotland,	Ms 18.5.20.
Liverpool,	City Museum,	Ms M 12024.
London,	British Museum,	Ms add. 12194.
		Ms add. 19768.
		Ms add. 28214.
		Ms add. 35285.
		Ms add. 47663.
		Ms Arundel 130.
		Ms Egerton 3272.
		Ms Harl. 1001.
		Ms Harl. 2911.
		Ms Harl. 2942.
		Ms Harl. 2945.
		Ms Harl. 2983.
		Ms Harl. 4951.
	Lambeth Palace,	Ms 438.
	St. Paul's,	Processional (no number).
Lucca,	Biblioteca del Capitolo,	Ms 609.
Madrid,	Biblioteca Nacionale,	Ms C 131.6.
Manchester,	Ryland's Library,	Ms 100.
		Ms 385.
Milan,	Biblioteca Trivulziana,	Ms a 14.
Norwich,	Museum Library,	Ms 49.158.926.
		Ms 158.926.4C.

Oxford,	Bodleian Library,	Ms Bodl. 637 (2024).
		Ms Buchanan e. 20.
		Ms Canonici lit. 291.
		Ms Canonici lit. 292.
		Ms Canonici lit. 308.
		Ms Douce 222.
		Ms e. mus. 126.
		Ms lat. liturg. e. 7 (32704).
		Ms lat. liturg. e. 8
		Ms lat. liturg. e. 18.
		Ms lat. liturg. f. 10.
		Ms liturg. 6 (30595).
		Ms liturg. 405.
		Ms liturg. 408 (30622).
		Ms liturg. d. 3 (31378).
		Ms misc. lit. 325.
		Ms Laud misc. 4.
		Ms Laud misc. 329.
		Ms Lyell 9.
		Ms Lyell 72.
		Ms Rawl. liturg. d. 4 (15846).
		Ms Rawl. liturg. e. 45 (15838).
		Ms Rawl. liturg. e. 46 (15843).
		Ms Rawl. liturg. e. 47 (15844).
		Ms Rawl. liturg. f. 35.
		Ms Selden Supra 37 (3415).
Oxford,	Corpus Christi College,	Ms 44.
	Jesus College,	Ms 10.
	St. Edmund's Hall,	Ms 1.
	St. John's College,	Ms 167.
Paris,	Bibliothèque Nationale,	Ms lat. 976.
		Ms lat. 990.
		Ms lat. 1017.
		Ms lat. 1120.
		Ms lat. 1121.
		Ms lat. 1236.
		Ms lat. 1240.
		Ms lat. 1301.
		Ms lat. 9970.
		Ms lat. 10511.
		Ms lat. 10579.
		Ms lat. 12050.
		Ms lat. 17436.
		Ms lat. 18044.
		Ms nouv. acq. 1235.
	Bibliothèque Ste-Geneviève,	Ms 111.
Rome,	Biblioteca Vaticana,	Ms 4750.
		Ms lat. 5319.

Rouen,	Archivo di S. Pietro,	Ms F 22.
	Bibliothèque de la Ville,	Ms 222 (A 551).
St. Gall,	Stiftsbibliothek,	Ms 448.
		Ms 486.
Salisbury,	Diocesan Registry Office,	Consuetudinary (no number).
	Sarum Cathedral,	Ms 175.
Sens,	Bibliothèque Municipale,	Ms 7.
Solesmes,	Monastery Scriptorum,	Metz Cathedral Ms 580 (photographs; Ms destroyed).
		Vich Ms (photographs; present owner unknown).
Stonyhurst,	Stonyhurst College,	Ms 41 (A VI 37).
		Ms 78.
Verdun,	Bibliothèque Municipale,	Ms 134.
		Ms 139.
		Ms 146.

BIBLIOGRAPHY

An asterisk indicates a separate entry in this listing.

Acta Sanctorum. Edited by Jesuit scholars. Third edition. Paris, 1863- .

Amalarius of Metz. *Opera Omnia Liturgica.* Edited by J. M. Hanssens as vols. CXXXVIII-CXL (1948-1950) of *Studi e Testi.* Rome, 1900- .

Analecta Hymnica Medii Aevi. Edited by G. M. Dreves, C. Blume and H. Bannister in 55 vols. Leipzig: Riesland, 1886-1922.

Antiphonale Missarum Sextuplex. Edited by René Jean Hesbert. Paris, 1935.

Antiphonale Monasticum. Edited by the Monks of Solesmes. Tournai: Desclée, 1939.

Antiphonale Sarisburiense. Edited by Walter Howard Frere. London, 1901-1925.

Antiphonario Visigotico Mozarabe de la Catedral de León. Edited in 2 vols. by Louis Brou and José Vives. Madrid, 1953, 1959.

Apel, Willi. *Gregorian Chant.* Bloomington: Indiana University Press, 1958.

Aurelian of Réomé. *Musica Disciplina.* Edited by Martin Gerbert in Vol. I of *Scriptores Ecclesiastici de Musica Sacra Potissimum.**

Bannister, H. M. "The Introduction of the Cultus of St. Anne into the West," *English Historical Review,* XVIII (1903), 107-112.

Batiffol, P. *Histoire du Bréviaire romain.* Paris, 1893.

Baudot, Jules. *The Roman Breviary.* London: Catholic Truth Society, 1909.

Bede. *De Temporum Ratione.* Edited by Jacques Paul Migne in Vol. XC of *Patrologia Latina.**

—, *Opera Historica.* Edited by C. Plummer with notes, in 2 vols. Oxford, 1896.

Bernhardi Cardinalis et Lateranensis Ecclesiae Prioris Ordo Officiorum Ecclesiae Lateranensis. Edited by J. Schlecht. Munich, 1916.

Bishop, Edmund. *Liturgica Historica* Oxford, 1918.

The Bobbio Missal. Edited by E. A. Lowe in Vols. LIII and LVIII (1917-1920) of the *Publications of the Henry Bradshaw Society.**

Breviarium ad Usum Sarum. Edited in 3 vols. by F. Proctor and Christopher Wordsworth. Cambridge, 1879-1886.

Bright, W. *Chapters of Early Church History.* London, 1878.

Brightman, Frank E. *The English Rite.* 2 vols. London, 1915.

Brou, Louis. "L'Antiphonaire grégorien au début du VIIIme siècle," in *Anuario Musical,* V (1950), 3-28.

Canones Apostolarum et Conciliorum. Edited by H. Bruns. Paris, 1893.

Catholic Encyclopedia. Edited by Charles Herbermann and others. 17 vols. and index. New York, 1907-1922.

Chailley, Jacques. *Histoire musicale du moyen age.* Paris: Presses Universitaires, 1950.

Chambers, J. D. *Divine Worship in England in the XIIIth and XIVth Centuries*. London, 1877.

Chavasse, Antoine. Le sacramentaire gélasien. Tournai: Desclée, 1958.

Cheetham, Samuel. *A History of the Christian Church during the First Six Centuries*. London: Macmillan, 1894.

Chomton, F. *Histoire de l'église Saint-Bénigne de Dijon*. Dijon, 1900.

Concilia Aevi Merovingici. Edited by F. Maassen for *Monumenta Germaniae Historica*. Hanover, 1893.

Concilia Magnae Britaniae et Hiberniae. Edited by David Wilkins in 4 vols. 1737.

Corbin, Solange. *La déposition liturgique du Christ au vendredi saint*. Paris: Société d'éditions "Les Belles lettres," 1960.

Council and Ecclesiastical Documents. Edited by A. Hadden and W. Stubbs. London, 1871.

The Customary of the Benedictine Monasteries of St. Augustine, Canterbury, and St. Peter, Westminster. Edited by Edward Thompson in Vol. XXIII (1902) of the *Publications of the Henry Bradshaw Society.**

The Customary of the Cathedral Priory of Norwich. Edited by J. Tolhurst in Vol. LXXXII (1948) of the *Publications of the Henry Bradshaw Society.**

Cyril of Scythopolis, *Life of Abbot Theodosius*. Edited by E. Schwartz in Vol. XLIX (1939) of the *Texte und Untersuchungen zur Geschichte der altchristlichen Literatur*. Leipzig, 1882-   .

—, *Life of St. Euthamius*. Edited by Jacques Paul Migne in Vol. CXIV of *Patrologia Graeca.**

DeBruyne, D. "L'origine des processions de la chandleur et des rogations..." in Revue Bénédictine, XXXIV (1922), 14-26.

Denholm-Young, N. *Handwriting in England and Wales*. Cardiff, 1954.

Dictionnaire d'archéologie chrétien et de liturgie. Edited by Fernand Cabrol and Henri Leclerc. Paris, 1903-1953.

Dictionnaire des antiquités grecques et romaines. Edited by E. Saglio. Paris, 1875-1912.

Dictionary of Christian Antiquities. Edited by William Smith and Samuel Cheetham. Toronto: Willing and Williamson, 1880.

Dizionario di Abbreviature Latine ed Italiane. Edited by Adriano Capelli. Milan: Hoepli, 1961.

DuCange, Charles. *Glossarium ... Mediae et Infimae Latinitatis*. Paris, 1678.

Duchesne, Louis. *Origines du culte chrétien*. Paris, 1889.

Dumoutet, E. *Le Christ selon la chair*. Beauchesne, 1932.

Dutripon, F. P. *Vulgatae ... Concordantiae*. Paris, 1838.

Early Bodleian Music. Edited in 3 vols. by E. Nicholson and C. Stainer. Oxford, 1901.

Enciclopedia Cattolica. Edited in 12 vols. by P. Paschini and others. Rome, 1949-1954.

Etheria. *Peregrinatio*. Edited by Louis Duchesne* in *Origines du culte chrétien*.

Eusebius Pamphilius. *Ecclesiastical History*. Translated from the Greek by C. F. Crusé. London: Bell and Sons, 1887.

Excerpta ex Ordinariis Germanicis. Edited by R. Stapper. Münster, 1936.

Ferretti, Paolo. *Esthétique grégorienne*. Tournai: Desclée, 1938.

Fortunatus. *Vita Germanii*. Edited by Jacques Paul Migne in vol. LXXXVIII of *Patrologia Latina.**

Frazer, J. G. *The Golden Bough*. One volume, abridged edition. New York: Macmillan, 1940.

Frere, Walter H. *Biblioteca Musico-liturgica*. 2 vols. London: Plainsong and Mediaeval Music Society, 1901-1932.

Froger, Jacques. *Les chants de la messe aux VIIIe et IXe siècles*. Paris: Desclée, 1950.

Gastoué, Amédée. *L'art grégorien*. Paris, 1911.
The Gelasian Sacramentary. Edited by H. A. Wilson. Oxford, 1894.
Gevaert, François A. *La melopée antique dans le chant*. Gand, 1895.
Golden Legend [Lombardica Historia]. William Caxton's translation has been edited in modern English by F. S. Ellis in 7 vols. London, 1900.
Graduale Romanum. Edited by the Monks of Solesmes. Solesmes, 1907.
Graduale Sarisburiense. Edited with an introduction by Walter H. Frere. London, 1894.
Le graduel de l'église cathédrale de Rouen au XIIIe siècle. Edited by H. Loriquet and others in 2 vols. Rouen, 1907.
Le Graduel romain: Les Sources. Edited by the Monks of Solesmes. Solesmes, 1957.
Gregorian Sacramentary. Edited by H. A. Wilson in Vol. XLIX (1915) of the *Publications of the Henry Bradshaw Society*.*
Gregory I. *Registrum Epistolarum*. Edited in 2 vols. by P. Ewald and M. Hartmann. Hanover, 1891, 1899.
Gregory of Tours. *Historia Francorum*. Edited by Jacques Paul Migne in Vol. LXXI of *Patrologia Latina*.*
—, *Liber de Gloria Confessorum*. Edited by Migne in Vol. LXXIX of *Patrologia Latina*.*
—, *Vita Sancti Aridii*. Edited by Migne in Vol. LXXI of *Patrologia Latina*.*
Gy, Pierre-Marie. "Collectaire, rituel, processionel," in *Revue des sciences philosophiques et théologiques*, XLIV (1960), 466 ff.

Hampson, R. T. *Medii Aevi Kalendarium*. London, 1841.
Harrison, Frank. *Music in Medieval Britain*. London: Routledge and Kegan Paul, 1958.
Heiligen-lexicon. Edited by Stadler and Heim. Augsburg, 1858-1882.
The Hereford Breviary Edited in 3 vols. by W. H. Frere and L. E. Brown in vols. XXVI, XL, XLVI (1904-1915) of the *Publications of the Henry Bradshaw Society*.*
Huglo, Michel. "Les antiennes de la procession des reliques: vestiges du chant 'Vieux Roman' dans le Pontifical," in *Revue grégorienne*, 1952, 136 ff.

Isidore of Seville. *De Ecclesiasticis Officiis*. Edited by Jacques Paul Migne in Vol. LXXXIII of *Patrologia Latina*.*
—, *Etymologiae*. Edited by Jacques Paul Migne in Vol. LXXXII of *Patrologia Latina*.*

John of Avranches. *Liber de Officiis Ecclesiasticis ad Maurilium Rotomagensis Archiepiscopus*. Edited by Jacques Paul Migne in Vol. CXLVII of *Patrologia Latina*.*
Justinian. *Novelae*. Edited by R. Schöll and W. Kroll in Vol. III (Berlin, 1928) of *Corpus Juris Civilis*.

Lanfranc. *Decreta*. Edited by David Knowles. London: Nelson and Sons, 1951.
Der Liber Ordinarius der Essener Stiftskirche. Edited by Franz Arens. Paderborn, 1908.
Liber Ordinarius Sancti Jacobi Leodiensis. Edited by Paul Volk. Münster, 1923.
Liber Pontificalis. Edited by Louis Duchesne in 2 vols. Paris, 1886-1892.
Liber Responsorialis. Edited by the Monks of Solesmes. Solesmes, 1895.
Lightfoot, Joseph B. *The Apostolic Fathers*. In 3 vols. London, 1885.
Lincoln Cathedral Statutes. Edited in 3 vols. by Henry Bradshaw and Christopher Wordsworth. London, 1892-1897.

Martène, Edmond. *De Antiquis Ecclesiae Ritibus.* In 3 vols. Rouen, 1700-1702. A later edition was published in Venice in 1738.

Martimort, Aimé-Georges. *L'Eglise en prière.* Paris: Desclée, 1961.

Maskell, William. *The Ancient Liturgy of the Church of England.* Third edition. Oxford: Oxford University Press, 1882.

Migne, Jacques Paul. *Dictionnaire des cérémonies.* In 3 vols. Paris, 1846-1847.

Mohlberg, Leo. *Liber Sacramentorum Romanae Aeclesiae Ordinis Anni Circuli.* Rome: Herder, 1927.

Morin, Germain. "Le plus ancien *comes* de l'église romaine," in *Revue Bénédictine,* XXVII (1910), 41-47.

Muratori, Ludovico. *Opere.* 13 vols. Arezzo, 1767-1773.

Die Musik in Geschichte und Gegenwart. Edited by Friedrich Blume. In 14 vols. Kassel: Bärenreiter, 1949-1967.

Nicolas, Harris. *The Chronology of History.* London: Longman, 1838.

L'ordinaire chartrain du XIIIe siècle. Edited by Yves Delaporte. Chartres, 1953.

L'ordinaire de Prémontré d'après des manuscrits du XIIe et XIIIe siècle. Edited by P. Lefèvre. Louvain, 1941.

Ordinaire et coutumier de l'église cathédrale de Bayeux. Edited by Ulysse Chevalier. Paris, 1903.

Ordinaires de l'église cathédral de Laon. Edited by Ulysse Chevalier. Paris, 1897.

Ordinaires de l'église Notre Dame d'Amiens par Raoul de Rouvroy. Edited by Georges Durand. Amiens, 1934.

The Ordinal of Barking Abbey. Edited by J. Tolhurst in Vols. LXV and LXVI (1927-1928) of the *Publications of the Henry Bradshaw Society.**

The Ordinal of St. Mary's, York. Edited by L. McLachlan and J. Tolhurst in Vols. LXXIII, LXXV, LXXXIV (1934, 1937, 1949-1950) of the *Publications of the Henry Bradshaw Society.**

Ordinale Exoniense. Edited by J. Dalton in Vols. XXXVII, XXXVIII, LXIII (1909-1926) of the *Publications of the Henry Bradshaw Society.**

Ordines Romani. Edited by M. Andrieu in 5 vols. Louvain, 1931-1961.

The Oxford Dictionary of the Christian Church. Edited by F. L. Cross. London: Oxford Press, 1957.

Paléographie musicale. Edited by the Monks of Solesmes. Tournai-Solesmes, 1889-   .

Pamelius [Jacques de Joigny]. *Liturgicon.* 2 vols. Cologne, 1571.

Patrologia Graeca. A corpus of Greek writers to 1439 edited under the direction of Jacques Paul Migne in 162 vols., Greek text and Latin translation. Paris, 1857-1866.

Patrologia Latina. A corpus of Latin ecclesiastical writers up to Innocent III (d. 1216) in 217 vols. edited under the direction of Jacques Paul Migne. Paris, 1844-1855.

Poitron, H. *La modalité grégorienne.* Tournai: Desclée, 1928.

Processionale ad Usum Insignis et Preclara Ecclesiae Sarum. Edited by W. G. Henderson. Leeds, 1882.

Processionale Monasticum. Edited by the Monks of Solesmes. Solesmes, 1893.

Processionale Sarum. London: Pynson, 1502. A single copy, printed on vellum, survives in the Library of St. John's College, Oxford.

Publications of the Henry Bradshaw Society. A series of editions of liturgical manuscripts, service books and illustrative documents mainly bearing upon the history of the Church of England. London, 1890-   .

Reese, Gustave. *Music in the Middle Ages*. New York: W. W. Norton, 1940.

Regularis Concordia. Edited by Thomas Symons. London: Nelson, 1952.

Repertorium Hymnologicum. Edited by Ulysse Chevalier in 6 vols. Louvain, 1892-1919.

Der Rheinauer Liber Ordinarius. Edited by A. Hänggi. Freiburg, 1957.

Rituale Graecorum. Edited by Jacques Goar. Paris, 1647.

Rituale Romanum. Prepared under the Pontificate of Paul V. Rome, 1614.

Rufinus of Aquilea. *Historia Ecclesiastica*. Edited by Jacques Paul Migne in Vol. XXI of *Patrologia Latina*.*

Das Sacramentarium Gregorianum nach dem Aachener Urexemplar. Edited by H. Lietzmann Münster, 1921.

Sacrosancta Concilia ad Regiam Editionem Exacta. Edited by Philippe Labbe. 1671-1673.

Sacrorum Conciliorum Nova et Amplissima Collectio. Edited in 31 vols. by Giovanni Mansi. 1758-1798.

St. Jerome. *Vita Hilarionis*. Edited by Jacques Paul Migne in Vol. XXIII of *Patrologia Latina*.*

The Sarum Breviary. Edited by F. Proctor and C. Wordsworth in 3 vols. Cambridge, 1879-1886.

The Sarum Missal. Edited by J. W. Legg. Oxford, 1916.

Sayles, G. O. *The Medieval Foundations of England*. London: Methuen, second edition, 1950.

Scriptores Ecclesiastici de Musica Sacra Potissimum. Edited by Martin Gerbert in 3 vols. Saint-Blasien, 1784.

Serrarius, N. *Sacri Peripatetici*. Cologne, 1607.

Sidonius Apollinaris. *Epistolae*. Edited by Jacques Paul Migne in Vol. LVIII of *Patrologia Latina*.*

Smits Van Waesberghe, J. *Gregorian Chant*. Stockholm, 1947.

Snow, Robert J. "The Old Roman Chant," in Willi Apel's* *Gregorian Chant* (1958), 484-505.

Sophocles, E. A. *Greek Lexicon of the Roman and Byzantine Periods*. Third edition, 1887.

Sozomen. *Ecclesiastical History*. Edited by Jacques Paul Migne in Vol. LXVII of *Patrologia Graeca*.*

Statuta et Consuetudines Ecclesiae Cathedralis Sarisberiensis. Edited by E. A. Dayman and W. H. Jones. Bath: privately printed, 1883.

Statutes of Lincoln Cathedral. Edited by Christopher Wordsworth. 2 vols. Cambridge, 1892-1897.

Statutes of the Cathedral Church of Sarum. Edited by Christopher Wordsworth and D. Macleane. Cambridge, 1915.

Stokes, G. T. *Ireland and the Anglo-Norman Church*. London, 1889.

Summary Catalogue of the Bodleian Library, Oxford. Published in 7 vols. Oxford, 1922-1953.

Suñol, Grégoire. *Introduction à la paléographie musicale grégorienne*. Paris: Desclée, 1935.

The Tracts of Clement Maydeston. Edited by Christopher Wordsworth in Vol. VII (1894) of the *Publications of the Henry Bradshaw Society*.*

Troparium Sequentiarum Nonantularum. Edited by Joseph Vecchi. Modena, 1955.

The Use of Sarum. Edited by Walter H. Frere in 2 vols. Cambridge, 1898-1901.

VanDijk, S. J. P., and Walker, J. *The Origins of the Modern Roman Liturgy*. London: Darton, Longman and Todd, 1960.

Vives, José. "Datacion del Antifonario Legionense," in *Hispania Sacra*, VIII (1955), 117-124.

Wagner, Peter. *Einführung in die gregorianischen Melodien*. Third edition, Leipzig, 1911.

Wagner, Peter. *Die Elemente des gregorianischen Gesanges. Regensburg*, 1917.

Watkins, E. I. *The Church in Council*. London: Darton, Longman and Todd, 1960.

Wordsworth, Christopher. *Ceremonies and Processions of the Cathedral Church of Salisbury*. Cambridge: University Press, 1901.

Wormold, F. *English Benedictine Calendars*. In 2 vols. London, 1938, 1946.

Wilson's English Martyrology. London, 1608.

The York Breviary. Edited by W. G. Henderson in Vol. LXXI (1880) of the *Publications of the Surtees Society*. Durham, 1835- .

The York Processional. Edited by W. G. Henderson in Vol. LXIII (1875) of the *Publications of the Surtees Society*. Durham, 1835-   .

Young, Karl. *The Drama of the Medieval Church*. In 2 vols. Oxford: The University Press, 1933.

INDEX